PROTECT YOURSELF
—WITH YOUR—
SNUBNOSE REVOLVER

GRANT CUNNINGHAM

**Protect Yourself With Your
SNUBNOSE REVOLVER**

By Grant Cunningham

Click or visit:
www.grantcunningham.com

CONTENTS

Each of these well-worn snubbies has been carried for personal protection, sometimes for many years!

INTRODUCTION

The snubnose revolver, also referred to as a "snubby" or the plural "snubbies," was once the predominant personal defense weapon in the United States. Over the last few decades, the snubby's role has been usurped by the subcompact autoloading pistol, and as a result the snubby is not nearly as common as it once was.

But that's not to say it isn't still around! All the major revolver manufacturers produce snubnose revolvers, even if they don't sell in the numbers they used to. You can find them on dealer shelves and in the hands of police officers (where they often serve as a backup gun to the officer's duty pistol), as well as in pocket and purse holsters, ankle holsters, and even sometimes on the belts of savvy concealed carriers.

In this day of polymer-framed, striker-fired autoloaders, you'd think the old-fashioned snubby would be distinctly obsolete. The death of the snubnose has been predicted for years, but they keep soldiering on because they just work!

The lawfully possessed and carried snubnose revolver isn't a magic talisman; it doesn't keep danger away from you or prevent you from doing things that increase your risk. It's a tool for a very small percentage of human interactions, but the consequences of those interactions can be dire to your existence. That's why tools like the snubby exist: to give you an even chance against someone who wants to do you immediate and grievous harm.

The snubby doesn't operate itself, either. Using the snubnose correctly, efficiently, and effectively requires a little work and commitment on your part. This book is dedicated to helping you do just that! With the information in these pages, plus a little work from you, you'll develop the judgement and physical skills you need to use your snubnose revolver to protect your life and the lives of your loved ones.

What exactly is a snubnose?

If you talk to several people, you'll get differing ideas of just what constitutes a snubby. Generally speaking, a classic snubnose is a small-framed, five- or six-shot revolver with a barrel of two inches or less in length. Examples include the Smith & Wesson Models 60, 36, and 42 (and variants, of which there are many); Colt Detective Special, Agent, and Cobra (all long discontinued but still favorites); Ruger SP101 and LCR; and other similar models from other manufacturers.

Admittedly those are somewhat arbitrary figures. Many people consider small-framed revolvers with three-inch barrels to be in the snubby family, and others consider larger-framed revolvers with two-inch barrels to be so as well. But in this book, I'll be using the term in its most classic sense and allow you the freedom to interpret the term however it pleases you!

Which caliber?

The most classic iteration of the snubby is chambered in .38 Special. You can find many snubbies chambered for the .357 Magnum round, which of course handles the Special as well; I usually consider them to be part of the family. Snubnose revolvers have been chambered in almost every conceivable revolver cartridge, along with a few made to take rimless autoloading cartridges.

Because this book is focused on defensive use of the snubby, most of the information centers on the .38/.357 models. This isn't to say that other calibers can't be used for self defense — they most assuredly have been — but most people choose one of the .38/.357 guns, which have the best combination of effectiveness and controllability. They're also the most commonly found on both the new and used markets.

The vast majority of the information in this book is equally applicable to other calibers. Even if you've got a snubby in .22 or .44, keep reading, because you'll find great information ahead!

THE UNIVERSAL SAFETY RULES

Like many other items in your home, firearms are very useful tools when handled properly, but quickly become dangerous when mishandled. Whenever you're handling your snubnose revolver, or whenever you're around people who are handling guns, it's important that you (and they) follow some rules to keep everyone safe.

Safety rules

Rules are behavioral guidelines that are universal: they are always applicable and should never be violated. While some specific or situational procedures might be required by the range you're using, you should always observe three universal rules whenever you're handling any firearm.

1. Always keep the muzzle pointed in a generally safe direction.

What is a generally safe direction? One in which, should the gun fire, you will not hurt someone else. On a shooting range, the berm or bullet trap behind the target is a generally safe direction, and depending on the surface the ground may be as well. There may be other generally safe directions which are location specific. Of course other shooters, staff or onlookers are never a generally safe direction!

2. Always keep your trigger finger outside of the trigger guard unless you're actually shooting.

The preferred place is on the frame above the trigger. In the case of the snubnose revolver, that means the frame space below the cylinder and above the trigger. It does not mean resting on the trigger guard itself!

3. Always remember you are in possession of a device that, if used recklessly or negligently, can injure or kill you or someone else.

This is the "big picture" of safety. It encompasses all those other safety rules you might see on posters and signs at the range: making sure of your target; making sure you know where the bullets will land; using the right ammunition for the gun; keeping your gun out of the hands of unauthorized users; etc. It is intended to instill in your mind an attitude about safety without providing an endless checklist of items to remember.

Safety procedures

Rules are universally applicable, while procedures are situational and help you implement the rules and keep yourself and other people safe. Procedures tend to be range- or activity-specific, and you may find some of them listed at your range.

SAFE AND READY STORAGE

Remember the third rule from the Universal Safety Rules section? "Always remember you are in possession of a device that, if used recklessly or negligently, can injure or kill you or someone else." As I explained, this is the rule that instills in your mind an attitude about safety and encompasses all those "other" rules you see in posters at shooting ranges.

One of the rules you might see on such a poster is to keep your gun locked up so others can't accidentally harm themselves or others. As a gun owner it's your job to keep your snubnose out of the reach of people who shouldn't have access to it, people you haven't authorized to have access. That responsibility accompanies the right to keep and bear arms, and it's one that unfortunately too few gun owners understand — until it's too late.

It's easy to find news stories where a child has been injured or killed because they found a gun and played with it. In almost every case, it's because the gun wasn't properly secured, and those cases are all preventable.

My general rule of thumb is that there are only two proper places for a firearm: on your person (or otherwise within your immediate control) or securely locked away. While Second Amendment purists lambast me for saying that, I believe it's the best rule for the responsible gun owner to follow.

The usual response I get is, "If it's locked up, it's no good for self defense!" That may have been true in the 1960s, but in the 21st century we have storage devices that not only make it easy to access a defensive handgun when needed, but also keep unauthorized people from gaining easy access.*

Quick-access safes

Today's snubby owner can pick from any number of quick-entry safes and lockboxes designed to give rapid access to a firearm yet keep it safe from all but a very determined person.

The method of access these devices employ varies a bit, but can be in the form of:

- a numeric keypad designed for easy entry of an access code even under stress
- a biometric lock, which reads the fingerprint of the authorized user and automatically unlocks
- an RFID system, which requires the presence of a coded bracelet, key fob, or card

Each method has its strengths and weaknesses, but any is better than a key- or traditional knob-type combination lock. Those old-fashioned locking systems are slower and harder to access in an emergency, which is the great innovation of the rapid-access products. They make it possible to keep the gun securely locked away yet sufficiently accessible in an emergency.

I recommend securely screwing or bolting the quick-access safe to a floor or wall, probably in your bedroom where it can be easily reached should your home be attacked at night. Doing this keeps the safe from being easily taken, but remember that a quick-access safe is not a burglar-resistant container. It's easily breached with normal hand tools. If someone is willing to destroy the box, they can reach your snubby!

If you're worried about theft, investing in a regular gun safe that's also been properly installed will offer significantly more theft protection. The quick-access safe is best thought of as restricting unauthorized access, not criminal access.

Home concealment products

Another option is to take advantage of some of the better home concealment products that have come onto the market recently. Companies such as Tactical Walls produce gun storage lockers that look like everyday objects hanging on your wall: mirrors, shelves, chalkboards, etc. While these require that you be handy with tools (or know someone who is) in order to install them, they do make it hard to determine that firearms are even present.

Keep in mind that most of these options are not designed to thwart physical access. If the person knows the firearms are there, the locking systems on most of these concealment products are easily defeated. The construction of these devices is also not intended to resist physical access. They are concealment products that mask the firearm in such a way that the casual observer (and even some less-than-casual observers) will pass them by.

When evaluating these options, eliminate from your consideration any that don't have some sort of latching or locking mechanism. Many of these products simply hinge or slide open. A toddler can get into them, and he doesn't even need to know the gun is there to accidentally stumble on the hiding place. A concealment product with a key, magnet, or RFID latch will keep small children out.

Hiding guns

The worst option is just hiding or stashing guns around the house. Many people put their guns on a high shelf or cabinet in the mistaken belief their children can't climb that high, or an intruder would never look there. Neither is the case!

Small children have an amazing ability to reach even the most inconveniently stored guns. Never underestimate the ability of a child to climb! Also don't underestimate their curiosity or observational skills. If you have a gun, no matter how careful you are to hide it from them, they probably know you have it and likely know where it is. After that, it's just a matter of figuring out how to get to it — and children often do, with tragic results.

Secure your snubby—don't just hide it.

A word about off-body carry and safety

At the beginning, I said the safest place for your snubby is on your person or otherwise within your immediate control. Many people choose to carry their snubnose revolver "off body": in a purse, briefcase, backpack, or other container. I'll cover this carry method in detail later, but for now I'll say the problem with it is that the container is not always on your person, and children find them fascinating.

Take, for example, the surprisingly common case of a woman shopping with her toddler. She puts her purse, which carries her defensive firearm, in the shopping cart with her child. When she turns her back, the child — being enamored, like all children are, with mommy's purse —finds the gun and pulls the trigger. Sometimes the bullet does nothing more than embarrass the mother, but in other cases the child has been hurt or killed. In more than one case, the child has accidentally killed the mother.

Worse yet are the myriad cases I've read where the mother comes home and puts her purse and gun on the aforementioned high shelf, where the child later finds it. In some cases, people have simply forgotten the purse contained a gun and left it on a coffee table or other easily accessible place. The results in both situations are often tragic.

If you choose off-body carry, you have to constantly remember you've put a gun into an insecure container and can never leave that container out of your sight and/or control. It's not a proper storage method and leaves a lot to be desired as a carry method (as mentioned, see the section on Concealed Carry for a more thorough examination of this carry method).

Never consider any off-body carry container a storage device. The rule about having the gun on your person or locked up still holds, perhaps even more so.

*— *Nothing is perfect, and there is no 100% infallible method to keep determined people away from your guns. Understand that any security device can be defeated, but that's no excuse not to use them!*

VIRTUES AND VICES OF THE SNUBBY

The virtues

The snubnose revolver was conceived as a personal-defense weapon. Some unknown person in a day long gone thought his revolver would be a lot more pocketable, and therefore more useful against the brigands of the time, if the barrel were bobbed. The result was intended to make the snubby what it still is: an easy-to-carry firearm to protect your life. Fast forward to the 21st century and we're still using that marvelous invention to protect lives!

The major defining feature of the snubnose revolver is its shortened barrel. The decrease in overall length makes it easy to carry in either a pocket* or on a belt. The reduced barrel length means it fits in a wider variety of concealment spaces, and is easier to retrieve from those spaces, than a longer-barreled revolver of the same model. Those attributes made the snubby the concealed-carry arm of choice before the term "concealed carry" was invented!

One of the snubby's unrecognized virtues is often thought to be a disadvantage: the diameter of the cylinder. Many people believe the bulge of the snubby's cylinder makes it more difficult to hide in concealed carry. I'll concede that even the smallest snubnose is thicker than a typical subcompact autoloading pistol, but the absolute width is only part of the story!

The snubby is a more "organic" shape; that is to say, its rounded contours make it concealable out of all proportion to its actual size. The smooth shape of the cylinder and grip frame seem to make covering garments glide over and around them, as opposed to being snagged by the squared-off corners of a semiautomatic pistol. I've found that the revolver is very easy to conceal under a wide range of conditions and clothing choices, oftentimes actually easier than a pistol of roughly the same dimensions.

The revolver's simplicity makes it a very efficient tool for self defense. There are no extraneous buttons or levers to push and no redundant safeties to defeat in order to fire a life-saving shot. Many autoloading pistols, for instance, have safeties and decockers that need to be operated to safely use the gun; the revolver has none of that nonsense. Autoloading pistols come in a variety of operating mechanisms, but if you've shot one snubby, you pretty much know how to shoot them all! The snubby's simplicity gives it a consistency that makes the gun easier for the novice to learn.

The snubby is easy to load and easy to unload: just open the cylinder and insert or eject the ammunition. This also makes it easy to verify if the snubby is loaded: simply opening the cylinder and looking at the chambers will tell you whether you need to load (or reload). Many beginning users feel more comfortable with this simple manual of arms than the more complex nature of the autoloading pistol.

Because the grip area isn't defined in size by the cartridges in a magazine, the snubby's grip is generally easier to fit to any given-sized hand than any other defensive firearm. Whether you have very small or very large hands, chances are you can find a grip to accommodate them — and changing the grip is a matter of finding a screwdriver and a couple minutes of spare time!

The snubnose revolver can be left loaded for a much longer period of time, without concern, than the autoloading pistol. There are no magazine springs to take a "set" and fail to feed. What's more, the snubby owner doesn't need to worry nearly as much about periodic cleaning and re-lubricating. This is because the operating power comes from the trigger finger, not a carefully balanced interaction of spring rates and recoil forces. Even after sitting for decades, you can fire the snubby revolver in confidence that all shots will ignite and exit the muzzle. That may not be true with the autoloading pistol!

Because of its resistance to neglect, the snubby makes an excellent choice for carry in dirty environments — such as in a pocket or purse.* Very often those kinds of "low-profile" carry locations are beset with lint and grit, the kind of debris that chokes an autoloading pistol. The snubby, however, thrives in those environments and remains reliable.

Is the snubby the perfect concealed-carry self-defense firearm? No, but then again, nothing is! The snubby has been with us for almost two centuries, however, because its combination of ease of use and ultimate reliability have endeared it to a great many users.

The vices

On the other hand, and despite being a popular self-defense arm from its earliest days, the snubby isn't without issues. Truth be told, no defensive firearm is without issues, and the snubby does have some deficiencies and limitations. It's always best to acknowledge limitations and find ways to train around them, which is what we'll be doing in the rest of this book!

What are some of those deficiencies?

To start, the short barrel that is the hallmark of the snubby means the sight radius — the distance between the front and rear sights — is much shorter than a regular revolver (or even a lot of small autoloading pistols). The shorter the sight radius, the more critical the alignment of the sights to an accurate precision shot. This doesn't mean the snubby isn't capable of great precision, because most models are mechanically accurate firearms. Many tests have been performed with a snubby shooting from a locked mechanical rest, and the results prove the design gives up very little accuracy to its larger brethren. Whether that mechanical accuracy is usable by the shooter is another question, because the short sight radius makes it more difficult to shoot to high levels of precision.

The snubby also suffers a bit because of its long, heavy trigger. Many snubbies combine that heavy trigger with a very light frame, which makes keeping the muzzle aligned on target more difficult. It's not unusual to see the trigger outweigh the entire gun by ten or 12 times! The force applied to make the trigger move also moves the gun, which in turn requires a very solid grasp to keep the gun from turning in your hands. The heavy trigger and long trigger travel make the snubby a more difficult gun to shoot to any given level of precision.

Speaking of keeping the gun under control, the snubby often comes from the factory with extremely small grips. Those "splinter" grips make controlling the gun very difficult, both in terms of countering the force applied to the trigger and dealing with the recoil. As I mentioned previously, grips are easily changed out for something more suitable, so this is a disadvantage only if you stick with the factory offerings.

The small size, light weight, and lack of energy-absorbing reciprocating parts mean the snubby has a higher recoil impulse for any given level of power. There are, for instance, revolvers chambered for the 9mm autopistol cartridge. When compared to a similarly sized semiautomatic pistol chambered for the same round, the revolver definitely has a sharper and more severe recoil impulse, which greatly affects the shooter's balance of speed and precision (a topic we'll delve into later.) It's tempting to load the snubby with the biggest, hottest ammunition available, but that's usually counterproductive to making rapid, multiple, accurate hits on target!

Along with the increase in perceived recoil comes an increase in muzzle blast: the concussion and flash that come from the end of the barrel. Many people find this the most distracting part of shooting the snubnose, and even with good ear protection it can be objectionable. It's not unusual to see the combination of recoil and muzzle blast result in a flinch, which must be trained away.

The short barrel of the snubby means bullets designed for longer-barreled revolvers may not perform as well. While this has been changing in recent years with the introduction of ammunition specifically tailored for the short barrels of concealed-carry firearms, care must still be taken in choosing defensive ammunition for the snubnose revolver.

Finally, the snubby is harder to reload than either the autoloading pistol or even a full-sized revolver. The comparison to the pistol is obvious: instead of a nice package that is inserted into a large opening, the revolver requires you to align five or six rounds with their individual chambers in the cylinder; in some cases, you have to do that several times to get the gun fully loaded.

But the comparison to larger revolvers is more subtle: with the small dimensions typical of snubbies, the cylinder doesn't open as far from the frame as larger revolvers. This means it's difficult to get rounds into the space, and speedloaders often get blocked by the upper part of the grips. Reloading the snubby efficiently requires a little more practice and attention to detail than any other commonly carried defensive handgun, including other revolvers.

Living with the snubby

It's important to acknowledge these issues up front. The vices of the snubnose are significant, and many people in the defensive training world feel the snubby isn't an ideal beginner's gun — a sentiment with which I concur. Put simply, the snubby is a very easy gun to shoot but a very difficult gun to shoot well!

What you'll find in the rest of this book are ways to take advantage of the snubby's virtues as well as ways to deal with its vices. You'll learn:

- how to effectively conceal the snubby and at the same time compensate for its vestigial sights
- how to grasp the gun to both deal with the recoil and operate the heavy trigger
- which ammunition works well in the short barrel
- reloading techniques that allow you to deal with both the threat and the difficulty of getting new ammunition into the small cylinder
- and a whole lot more!

Everything that follows is designed from the ground up to help you live with the virtues and vices of the snubnose. I don't pull any punches; I acknowledge the limitations and then show you ways around them. You'll learn how to use the snubby to its full advantage to protect your life, or the lives of your loved ones, from those who would harm you.

The snubnose revolver has been doing that job proudly for many generations before us, and will likely continue to do so for many generations to follow!

— A snubnose revolver should always be carried in a holster, and never loose in a pocket or purse!

MANUAL OF ARMS

The term "Manual of Arms" comes from the early days of firearms, when shooting a gun was a complicated affair requiring that many steps be done in a specific order. Those steps were written down in a manual for reference by the operator. Today it refers to the way in which a specific gun is handled: how it's loaded and unloaded, for example, or how safety or fire mechanisms are operated.

Double-action revolvers in general, and the snubnose in particular, have generally hewn to a fairly consistent pattern of operation. Such is not the case with the autoloading pistol, which is available in a wide variety of operating systems and control layouts, each of which can have substantial effects on how you train, practice, and use it in a defensive encounter.

But the manual of arms for the revolver is pretty much the same from model to model and manufacturer to manufacturer. For instance, though there are some slight differences in how the cylinder latch operates between brands, by and large if you pick up one revolver, it will be nearly identical to the last. If, for instance, you own a Ruger, you can readily figure out how a Colt works and vice-versa.

Operating Controls

Trigger: the trigger on a double-action revolver always has a longer, heavier travel to fire a round than a typical semiautomatic pistol. It also doesn't "reset" to a shorter throw like a lot of pistols do. The trigger has to be allowed to completely reset for the next shot.

Hammer: all snubnose revolvers currently on the market have a hammer of some sort. The hammer may be exposed, with a spur to allow it to be cocked to a short single action; exposed but spurless, operating in double-action mode only; or "hammerless", which is a slight misnomer for a snubby in which the hammer is concealed (such as the Smith & Wesson Centennial series of snubbies).

Cylinder Latch: the cylinder latch allows the cylinder to be swung out and away from the frame for loading, reloading, or unloading. On the vast majority of snubnose revolvers, the latch is on the left side of the gun below the hammer. The only common exception — and it's not all that common — is the Dan Wesson revolver, on which the cylinder latch is in front of the cylinder, on the left side of the frame. On a Smith & Wesson snubby, the cylinder latch is pushed forward, toward the muzzle, to open the cylinder. On a Colt, the latch is pulled backward, while on a Ruger the latch is pushed in toward the opposite side of the gun. On the aforementioned Dan Wesson revolver, it is pushed downward.

Ejector Rod: the ejector rod is what you push to eject spent (empty) cartridge casings from the cylinder. In all cases, the ejector rod is pushed in, toward the cylinder, to operate. On all but the newer Ruger revolvers, the ejector rod spins when the cylinder is rotated. On modern Rugers, the ejector rod remains stationary. Older Ruger snubbies, such as the Speed-Six model, have a rotating ejector rod.

Loading and Unloading

I recommend you handle your snubby in as consistent a manner as possible. This reduces training time and effort, with the additional benefit of making you safer. As you'll see when we get to the section on Reloading the snubby, that procedure has a lot in common with administrative loading. Doing them both in the same way all the time makes it easier to learn to reload during an emergency, because you're using skills you've already practiced.

In the instructions that follow, I'm assuming you're a right-handed person. If you're left-handed, for the most part you can simply reverse or mirror the movements.

Loading the snubby
To load the snubnose, turn your support hand palm-up. Put the trigger guard in your palm with the cylinder itself positioned between your thumb (on one side of the cylinder) and the forefinger and middle finger on the other side.

Press the cylinder release with your shooting-hand thumb and at the same time push the cylinder open with your fingers. As the cylinder opens, your forefinger and middle finger will push through the frame.

Immobilize the cylinder in the fully open position between your thumb and the other fingers.

Point the muzzle straight at the sky and strike the ejector rod with the palm of your shooting hand. This clears any spent brass and ensures that the ejector is working and the ejector "star" is properly seated.

Point the muzzle at the ground. This involves rotating your wrist and forearm. Don't worry if the muzzle isn't exactly and precisely vertical. Just point it at the ground as much as you comfortably can.

Your shooting hand now inserts the new rounds into the chambers.

Get a firing grip on the gun with your shooting hand, making sure your finger is off the trigger, and close the cylinder like you would a book.

If you're ready to start shooting, get a two-handed grasp with the support hand. If not, put the snubby into the holster (or wherever it's going to be staged).

Unloading the snubnose

Many people will suggest you unload your snubnose in the same way you prepare to reload it. I'm not of that mind. Administratively unloading the snubby is done for safe storage purposes or, more commonly, to prepare it for cleaning and maintenance. I prefer to make the unloading procedure as distinctly separate as possible, to minimize the chances of reflexively inserting live ammunition into the chambers.

Start with the snubby sitting in your support hand and your thumb and forefinger cradling the cylinder. Press the cylinder latch with your shooting hand and open the cylinder.

Like the loading procedure, the cylinder should be immobilized between your thumb and forefinger.

Here's where the procedure becomes unique: hold your shooting hand under the cylinder as the muzzle is pointed toward the sky and catch the rounds that fall out of the chambers.

At the same time, press the ejector rod with the thumb of your support hand. This should extract any spent brass. Allow the ejector rod to retract.

If there were spent casings that didn't fall clear, use your shooting hand to pull them free. Put the live ammunition and spent brass somewhere convenient.

Point the muzzle at the ground and look through each chamber to verify it is empty. Feel the mouth of each chamber with the fingers of your shooting hand as a double-check that the gun is truly unloaded.

Close the cylinder. You're ready to store the snubby in an appropriately secure place or perform cleaning and maintenance.

Special note if you're preparing to clean your snubnose

Put the revolver down and take the ammunition you just ejected out of the room; at the very least, remove it from the immediate area to reduce the chances of it accidentally finding its way back into the cylinder. (You may be chuckling or even dismissive of this, but hardly a week goes by that I don't hear of an accident with a supposedly unloaded gun. It's surprisingly easy to stick a live round into a chamber if you're even momentarily distracted. Gun safety is no place to take shortcuts!)

When you've removed the ammunition from the area, repeat the unloading procedure as a double-check that the gun is truly unloaded. You can now clean and maintain your snubby in a safe environment!

DEFENSIVE AMMUNITION FOR THE SNUBNOSE

The snubnose revolver is not a target pistol and it's not a hunting gun. It's a defensive tool and always has been, and because of that it should be carried with ammunition suitable for the task of stopping an attacker — and the sooner that happens, the better for everyone concerned!

Let's look at the differences between practice or range ammunition and defensive ammo.

Practice ammunition is generally the cheapest type of ammo you can buy for use in practice and training. It's almost invariably a solid lead bullet, or perhaps a solid lead bullet with a brass jacket, which are the least expensive bullet types to make and load. Practice ammunition isn't less lethal or less dangerous, but it is inadequate to reliably stop a determined attacker quickly. You use it in practice and training because it's cheap and easy to find but still accurate and reliable. Many people refer to practice ammunition as "ball ammo," from an old term for the solid round projectile that was used in muzzle-loading rifles. It's also often called "FMJ," which stands for full metal jacket over a solid lead core.

Defensive ammunition (some people call it "carry ammo") usually has a bullet featuring a hollow-point design that expands on impact with an adversary. The expansion tends to slow the bullet down so it's less likely to pass through and injure an innocent person on the other side of your attacker, while at the same time making a larger wound that is more likely to cause incapacitation. The performance of defensive ammunition means you're less likely to need to shoot your attacker as many times as you would with less effective ammunition. The nature of defensive ammunition also means the bullets are less likely to ricochet should you miss the target, or if they should somehow pass through the target and hit a solid surface.

Defensive ammunition is almost always significantly more expensive than plain ball or FMJ ammunition, which is why it's not usually recommended for regular practice or training. It's also harder to find on store shelves, so availability alone reduces its suitability for extended shooting.

How defensive ammunition works

When the hollow-point defensive bullet enters the target its forward momentum, coupled with the viscous nature of the human body, causes the bullet to immediately start expanding or increasing in diameter. This "parachute" effect slows the bullet down slightly and makes it more difficult to pass through matter, which is why it's less likely to exit the target: it uses up all its energy trying to get through the target. At the same time, the increased diameter results in a larger hole and greater tissue damage, increasing blood loss and affecting the operation of internal organs. That combination is far more likely to cause incapacitation, which means that your attacker stops attacking you.

Heavy and slow or light and fast?
As I've often said, the bullet has to get to something the body finds immediately important and it has to do rapid and significant damage to that thing once it arrives. As it happens, there is a range of ways to do both of those things, which is why so many bullet choices are on the market today!

You'll hear arguments from those who believe that light and fast bullets result in faster incapacitation, while the proponents of heavier/slower bullets believe they have greater "knockdown power." In general, your best results are likely to come from bullets in the middle of the weight and velocity ranges for the caliber. Extremely light bullets tend to produce shallow wounds (they don't always reach important things), while very heavy bullets tend not to do a lot of damage when they arrive (and they often exit the target without having done a lot of work).

My usual recommendation is to pick a quality bullet from a major manufacturer in the middle of the weight range for the caliber and you'll generally be in good shape. However, the snubnose revolver adds its own complication to the issue: barrel length.

Effects of the short barrel
In general, the longer the barrel, the more velocity the cartridge will generate (up to a certain limit, of course). The shorter the barrel, the less velocity

you're likely to get. The problem is that expanding bullets tend to be velocity sensitive. The more slowly the bullet travels, the less likely it is to expand as designed and therefore the less likely it is to incapacitate your attacker.

In the past, most defensive revolver ammunition was designed for what was termed "service length" barrels: four to six inches in length, which were the guns police routinely carried in their service. Those longer barrels gave plenty of time for the gunpowder to completely combust and drive the bullet to the desired velocity. In the very short snubby barrels that didn't always happen, and ammunition often under-performed.

Things are different today! Since no police agencies issue revolvers, and few people carry revolvers with four- or six-inch barrels, defensive ammunition manufacturers have turned their design prowess to making ammunition that works well out of the now-more-common snubnose barrels. As a result, we have much better defensive ammunition than ever before!

That's why my recommendation for snubbies is a little different: pick a major manufacturer's modern hollow-point bullet that has been specifically designed to expand out of a short barrel. Speer was the first to make such specially tailored defensive ammunition, but in recent years other manufacturers have also optimized their cartridge designs for snubby use.

Special or magnum?

Any discussion of defensive ammunition would be incomplete without mention of the choice between the classic .38 Special and the vaunted .357 Magnum (for those guns that chamber both, of course). You might not be aware of it, but this discussion has partisans who argue quite vehemently!

The arguments revolve around the supposed power of the .357 Magnum, whose advocates claim that "nothing drops bad guys" as well as the .357, and often point to poorly researched "one-shot stop" data from the 1980s to prove their point. The Special advocates, on the other hand, take their opinions from the days before chronographs were common. They counter that the extra power of the Magnum is "wasted" from a short barrel, with the result that the .357 rounds don't actually give any better performance out of a snubby but do produce more recoil and muzzle flash.

What is the common denominator between the two opinions? If you've read carefully, you'll note that the arguments are both old. They're based on assumptions made decades ago, before we had the kind of information and real-world data we have today!

Here's the reality in the 21st century: for my money, the best information we have about real-world shooting results comes from the research of Greg Ellifritz, a police officer in Ohio. He's looked at thousands of shootings over the years and carefully compiled the information* into a comprehensive look at ammunition performance. In his data, the .357 Magnum does in fact result in slightly faster incapacitation, with slightly fewer rounds being fired than the .38 Special.

But that's not the whole story. The difference in performance is very close to the expected margin of error in the study; in other words, it may or may not be slightly better. What isn't arguable, however, is that the Magnum does produce substantially greater recoil, muzzle flip, and muzzle blast than the Special. This translates to being harder to control and slower consecutive shots.

It's the "consecutive shots" part that is important. What's most interesting from Ellifritz's study is that the major determinant factor in how quickly an attacker stopped was how many rounds the defender was able to land on target. Regardless of the caliber of the gun, the more shots that landed accurately on target, the more quickly and reliably the attacker was stopped.

If you're forced to shoot an attacker, your best defense is to deliver rapid, multiple, accurate rounds on target. The Magnum makes that significantly more difficult to do and without a correspondingly significant increase in effectiveness. For my money, then, I'd much rather have a gun that I can shoot faster and more reliably when I really need to. Despite having lots of experience with Magnum handguns, I'll pick a good .38 Special load every time, and I strongly recommend that you do as well!

What Is +P ammunition?

Remember I said a bullet has to get to something important and do damage to that thing when it gets there? Well, sometimes rounds fall just short of that ideal. A modest increase in power often gives the round just enough to get it "over the hump." This is a fact that ammunition manufacturers learned a long time ago.

But it's not quite that simple. There are pressure standards for ammunition to maintain safety, and increasing the power almost certainly results in higher pressures. The .357 Magnum, for instance, operates at a little over twice the pressure of the .38 Special to reach its much higher velocities!

Ammunition makers soon discovered that if they could increase the pressure of the round just a little, they'd get enough additional power to make the bullet perform the way it needed to perform. The Sporting Arms and Ammunition Manufacturers Institute (SAAMI), which is the standards group that sets ammunition pressure limits, invented a new designation for rounds that were a little over the standard pressure limits and called them "+P" loads.

The +P designation refers to ammunition that is loaded to those slightly increased pressures and has increased velocity as a result. Manufacturers usually caution not to use this "hotter" ammunition in antique guns or firearms that aren't designed to take the pressure, but virtually all modern snubnose revolvers safely handle the +P loads.

As it happens, today's ammunition manufacturers have made good use of that extra performance the +P limits give them. The .38 Special +P defensive ammunition available today performs superbly in "real world" applications yet has mild recoil and as a result is much easier to control than the fire-breathing .357 Magnum.

Defensive ammunition recommendations

Keep in mind that ammunition companies discontinue specific loads from time to time. As I write this (late 2016), these are my recommendations for currently available defensive ammunition. All have good track records in real-life shootings and have been designed specifically for self defense when fired out of a snubnose revolver.

Speer Gold Dot, 135-grain .38 Special +P jacketed hollow-point: This is arguably the best choice in defensive ammunition for the snubby. It was the first purpose-built round for self defense and short barrels, and remains the standard against which all others are judged. Because of its police origins, it has been studied more than any other and has performed amazingly well over many shootings and many years.

Winchester PDX-1, 130-grain .38 Special +P jacketed hollow-point: A relative newcomer compared to the Speer offering, but it has racked up a significant reputation of its own. Again, derived from Winchester's police ammunition experience and a very consistent performer over a wide range of conditions.

Remington HTP, 158-grain .38 Special +P lead hollow-point: Back before we had the new purpose-made short-barrel ammunition, police agencies looked for any ammo that would work in both the patrol officers' duty revolvers and the snubbies issued to detectives. The result was this +P all-lead semi-wadcutter hollow-point. While its performance is not as stellar as the more modern loads listed above, it remains a viable choice for some snubbies and some shooters.

(I say 'some' because many older snubnose revolvers will not shoot to point-of-aim with the newer, lighter bullets. On the other hand, some shooters don't like the increased recoil of this heavier load.)

While it would not be my first choice, it's still a much better option than some of the ultra-light defensive ammunition being sold today. Because of its wide use in law enforcement, it was offered by all the major ammunition manufacturers for decades, but today Remington is the only company regularly producing this classic load.

* — You can read Greg Ellifritz's study at www.activeresponsetraining.net/an-alternate-look-at-handgun-stopping-power

THE GOAL OF DEFENSIVE SHOOTING

The snubnose revolver (or any firearm, really) is a special-purpose tool suitable for a very limited range of interpersonal conflicts: those where an immediate and otherwise unavoidable danger of death or grave bodily harm to you or other innocent people exists. The firearm is not a safety device, in the sense that it prevents things from happening to you;. It's a response tool that allows you an efficient means of surviving a lethal incident in which shooting is the correct response.

I say it that way because there are lethal incidents where shooting is not the correct response. Automobile crashes and house fires are certainly lethal incidents, but shooting isn't an appropriate way to deal with them! The kind of lethal response we're talking about is one in which another human being is doing something to cause you (or an innocent) grievous bodily harm.

The primary goal of defensive shooting, then, is to stop the threat from harming, or continuing to harm, you or others. Your attacker may in fact die as the result of your lawful and ethical use of lethal force, but that isn't the goal. Stopping him from hurting you, as reliably or as predictably as possible, is the reason you have your snubnose revolver.

In this book, we're going to look at self defense from the "worst-case scenario": the surprise attack, the one you did not see coming before it happened, and which happens outside of arm's length.

Self defense = skills + knowledge

Effectively defending yourself with a snubby requires both physical shooting skills and some knowledge about the use of force (the latter being beyond the scope of this book*). As a private citizen carrying or using a firearm for self defense, you want to be able to stop a lethal attack, not to serve as law enforcement or extract any sort of "payback." **

This book primarily focuses on the skills you need to know in order to defend yourself with your snubnose revolver. As it happens, those skills aren't as exotic as some people make them out to be! In the vast majority of cases, the shooting problems aren't terribly difficult for someone with a passing knowledge of shooting concepts. You certainly don't need to be some super-competitive shooter to protect your life, as tens of thousands of ordinary men and women prove every year.

You should have a practiced skill set that reflects the likely kinds of shooting issues you might encounter. These skills will ideally be ones that work well with your body's natural threat reactions and make the best use of your defensive resources (time, ammunition, energy, and space). At the same time, they should be skills that you can practice easily and frequently without the need to travel to a specially equipped range facility. That's exactly what you'll learn in the rest of this book!

Mindset

First, you need to make a decision: that your own life and the lives of your loved ones are worth protecting. This isn't an easy decision for some people because it carries with it three unpleasant realizations: first, that you're mortal and can die prematurely. Second, that evil people who do unspeakable things to innocent human beings exist in this world; and finally, that your defensive response may result in the death of another human being.

It's not easy to face the fact that you're going to die. Like many people, you may put off important things like wills and end-of-life instructions because it's not pleasant to contemplate your own demise. But it's important to face up to this fact, because the corollary to it is the fact that you can be killed prematurely and without warning. It's the premature death at the hands of another person that you want to prevent, but a paralyzing fear of death will keep you from even thinking about it — let alone planning to prevent it. It's ironic, really: you need to accept the reality of your own mortality before you can decide to forestall it as long as possible!

The second realization is that not everyone is like you. I suspect you and I have a lot in common: I grew up in a typical American family surrounded by honest, hard-working people of all social positions. We didn't often run into people who lived a life of crime or who looked at other people as resources to be exploited. The idea that someone would actually see another human being as simply a crop to be harvested was so beyond my experience that my first encounter with a human predator stunned me.

In the years since I've learned that such a realization stuns most normal people, to the extent that they can't defend themselves when they suddenly come face to face with evil.

You must understand and accept that there are in fact evil people in this world who want to hurt you. Only when you acknowledge this reality will you be able to learn how to respond appropriately when faced with someone intent on harming you or your loved ones.

Finally, you have to come to grips with the possibility that defending yourself with a firearm may result in the death of another human being. Evil though he (or she) may be, hurting another human being is usually something those of us raised in polite society are loathe to do. Yet we must do it if we're to keep evil from ending our own lives. By attacking you, by violating you, the evil predator has forfeited his own life. He made that decision when he got you in his sights; it was part of his risk/reward calculation. If you hesitate because of a completely understandable reticence to hurt others, you may lose the encounter and possibly your life.

This isn't to say we intend to kill someone, you understand, because our goal isn't his death: the goal is stopping the attack. Death is sometimes an inevitable by-product of what it takes to physically stop someone who is determined to follow a certain path.

Live for others

Over the years, I've met many people who say they couldn't possibly kill another person to save themselves. This reflects back on the last point I made above: they don't want to face the reality that their defensive actions may prove lethal to their attacker, even if that was not their express intention.

But when I ask them if they'd kill someone who was attacking their children, their attitude suddenly changes: of course they would! Their protective instincts come to the surface, and they admit they'd do anything — including sacrificing their own life — to save their kids. This is as it should be.

If you're hesitant about the prospect of using deadly force to protect your life, I'd like you to consider this point: your children and the rest of your loved ones need you. How would your children make it through the tough times of their lives without your love, guidance, and protection? How much pain will your spouse or your parents or your siblings suffer from losing you? How much good will not get done in this world because someone took you from it prematurely?

You don't live in a vacuum or a world apart from others. People need you, depend on you, and cherish you. Depriving them of your presence can do irreparable damage to them, and in some cases might even alter their lives irretrievably. You're not saving your own life out of narcissism or selfishness — you're saving it so you can help others live their lives, too. The person who attacks you with the intention of harming or killing you is the selfish one, the one who hurts others through you. By defending yourself, you deny him his prize and save others from the cascading harm he might cause.

If you can't live for yourself, live for the others in your life.

Effective skills are relevant skills

If you're attacked and forced to use your snubnose revolver to defend your life, you have to face certain physical realities. Those realities affect how and what you train.

The closest thing we have to a certainty in this field is that our bodies react in specific and largely predictable ways when they sense a lethal threat. We've evolved over millennia to survive against even apex predators, and we've been able to do so because our brains are wired to detect and react to things that might kill us.

Those reactions affect how you use tools, and in particular the snubnose revolver. As a result, the techniques you use for manipulation and employment of the snubby should, to the greatest degree possible, work with how your body wants to react.

In the rest of this book, you'll see how each of the techniques you're learning is congruent with what your body does naturally. Anything not congruent with your natural threat reactions is harder to learn, harder to recall, and less likely to be used when your body goes into a full-threat alarm reaction. Why bother with those when you can instead learn things that do work with your body's natural reactions? That's what the rest of this book is about!

* — *I heartily recommend two books to further your education with regard to the legal aspects of the use of deadly force. The first is* **Deadly Force: Understanding Your Right to Self Defense** *by Massad Ayoob. It's a very readable general guide to the concept of self defense and how the legal system looks at the use of lethal force. The second is* **The Law of Self Defense: The Indispensable Guide for the Armed Citizen, 3rd Edition** *by attorney Andrew Branca. It is the most comprehensive guide to self defense law outside of a law library and includes state-specific analysis of the laws surrounding self defense and the use of force.*

** — *While in some rare states or localities the use of force to protect property is enshrined in statute, that's not what we'll be talking about in this book. Here, we're concerned with protecting your own life or the lives of other innocents against those who would harm them directly.*

THE LEAST UNDERSTOOD WORD IN SELF DEFENSE

One of the most important ideas in all of defensive training is context. Context means related to, or from an environment where, a concept can be used or understood. Everything has a context in which it makes sense and in which it's usable, including defensive shooting skills, techniques, and concepts.

This book looks at private-sector self defense — you protecting your own life, or the lives of your loved ones — in contrast to a military context, a law enforcement context, or a competition shooting context. The rules of engagement, the circumstances under which force is used, and the skills and techniques vary in each of those contexts. What is appropriate for or important to a soldier or a cop or a competitive shooter is often very different from what's important to you and your family!

Of course some overlap exists because much of the actual physical shooting part of each job is similar. In other words, operating a trigger is the same whether you're scared because a mugger is attacking you or you're scared because an enemy soldier is attacking you. Some technique is in fact interchangeable. But knowing how to evaluate each technique for its application in your context is important to being able to spot when something isn't applicable to the job you need to do. You make that evaluation by understanding the context where something makes sense, and how that context is different than yours.

Everything you'll learn in this book is based on the context of the worst-case scenario for the average citizen: the ambush. That's the term for the typical attack on a private citizen, an attack you did not know was coming ahead of time and to which shooting is the correct response. That is the context of private sector self defense.

Do your skills match your life?

Ignoring the context of a skill can result in poor defensive training decisions. Take, for example, reloading the handgun. In a competition context, where most reloading techniques come from, no one is shooting back. Regardless of the amount of stress (which in competition is nothing more than simple performance anxiety), the body's natural threat reactions have not been activated. Because of that reality, the competitive shooter's reloading technique has been maximized for speed under the conditions it's likely to be used: on a nice, flat range with obstructions that have been identified beforehand and against a target that doesn't move.

Now take those same skills and apply them to your world. Your attacker is trying to hurt you; your attention and vision are focused on your attacker; the ground under the smooth soles of your dress shoes is wet, uneven, and strewn with trash; it's dark; and the rain makes the gun and your spare ammunition slippery. The reloading technique optimized for speed under the ideal conditions of a shooting match might result in a botched reload, while a technique that's slightly slower but optimized for reliability under adverse conditions will succeed. The difference is in the context of application, and it matters.

Context is a very useful tool to help evaluate techniques and ideas. The context of the material in this book is private sector self defense against a surprise attack, and everything you're going to learn is optimized for that task — your task!

WHAT ARE YOU EXPECTING?

Many things in this world are possible, in the sense that the laws of physics do not preclude them. But that doesn't mean all of those things are equally likely to occur! Many, perhaps most, of the things that are possible are exceedingly unlikely to happen.

I've used this example in my classes for years (and only recently discovered it was the plot of a popular movie*): North Korean paratroopers taking over a shopping mall. It's certainly possible, in the sense that the laws of physics do not prevent North Koreans from being paratroopers, but I think you can agree it's not at all likely. In fact, it is for all intents and purposes a fantasy scenario.

Let's say, though, that you didn't differentiate between likely and possible and spent your time preparing and training for the arrival of those enemy paratroopers. That's time, energy, and money that couldn't be used to prepare for the far more likely event of a carjacking or mugging. The paratroopers and the carjacker have nothing in common. The proper response for each is completely different, and by spending your time preparing for the unlikely event, you've left yourself vulnerable to the more likely threat.

It's a contrived comparison, of course, but it serves to illustrate the concepts of possibility, plausibility, and likelihood.

The Three States of Expectation

For our purposes, there are three states of expectation for any kind of event, and understanding their relationship will help you make better protection decisions.

As I said in the paratrooper example, Possible events are all those things that could happen merely because the laws of physics allow them. Life has a huge range of possibilities, some of which are likely and some of which aren't. It's useful to think of it this way: everything that could happen is possible, but not everything that's possible could really happen!

Likely events, on the other hand, are those that you can reasonably expect to face. They have some mathematical certainty to them, largely because they happen just often enough that we can establish some level of probability as to their occurrence. In fact, probable is another way to express the concept of likelihood. They are events that we can have some expectation of happening. (It can also refer to the skills for which there is some expectation of need.)

A third level of expectation sits between what is merely possible and what is actually likely. These are events we can conclude could happen because there is some historical basis for them happening. In other words, while they don't happen often enough to be certain or even mathematically likely, they've happened often enough that they could reasonably be believed to occur in your life. They may also be the logical expected result of some foreseeable if not common combination of events. These events exist in the Plausible state of expectation: things that could believably occur to you because they have or could be expected to.

Why understanding expectation is important

Getting back to our paratrooper example, it should be self evident that no one has an unlimited amount of time, energy, money, and interest to train for everything that is possible. Something has to give: if you train and equip for the paratroopers, that's time/money/effort/interest you can't use to prepare for burglars. You need to prioritize what you do in order to establish a way of deciding what skills to learn and practice.

It makes sense to first prepare for those events that fall into the Likely pile. Once you've equipped yourself and developed the skills to deal with those, you can expand the application of your core skills to Plausible events. If an event falls outside of the Plausible category, it's merely a possibility and shouldn't merit much (if any) of your preparation resources.

Think of it like budgeting: you can't afford everything, so you need to decide what's important to you and spend your funds on those things first. It's the same idea.

Skills have states of expectation too

So far we've been talking about events or incidents: things that happen to you and affect what you train for. They help you budget your preparation resources: time, money, energy, and interest.

Your expectation of using a particular skill also falls into one of the states. There are skills you're likely to need, skills you might plausibly need, and skills that fall into the range of merely possible (or, as I like to refer to it, "fantasyland"). Training in skills that aren't Likely or Plausible is a waste of your preparation resources.

For instance, reloading the snubnose revolver isn't a Likely skill. It's extremely difficult to find instances in private sector self defense where people needed to reload their guns, and nearly impossible to find one where the reload had an effect on the outcome of the incident. It's just not a skill people actually use, and yet it takes up a lot of time in most defensive shooting courses. I've seen instructors spend the better part of an hour on the topic, teaching several different reloading methods and doing specialized reloading drills, all for a skill that students will probably never need. This valuable and expensive instructional time could have been better used to teach skills the students are far more likely to need!

Reloading in general, then, doesn't neatly fall into the Plausible category, because there's little historical expectation of need. But reloading the snubnose revolver in particular might, because of a combination of foreseeable events: the smaller ammunition capacity of the typical snubby combined with a known increase in the number of multiple-assailant crimes. We can therefore justify devoting slightly more of our preparation (training) resources in learning how to do it efficiently and reliably than we might if we were considering a high-capacity autoloading pistol. It's still not likely, but the combination of capacity and circumstances make it a little more plausible.

Once you've mastered the Likely shooting skills, you can expand the range of application to include Plausible situations. There are no "advanced" defensive shooting skills, there are simply advanced applications of the fundamental skills you'll learn in the rest of this book.

* — *No, really: I had no idea this was a movie plot! I thought I was just unusually and uniquely creative when I came up with the storyline. Perhaps instead of writing self-defense books, I should write movie scripts?*

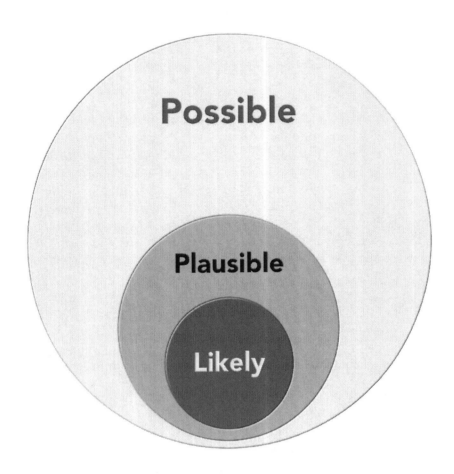

BEING EFFICIENT

One definition of efficiency is "the ability to do something or produce something without wasting materials, time, or energy." In other words, making the best use of available resources to achieve a specific goal (or perform a specific task).

Efficiency in training

When we consider efficiency in defensive shooting, we talk about being efficient in both training and response. You should guard your training resources jealously: your time, energy, personal interest, and money are all important resources that help you achieve your goals. None are infinite! Even if you are rich beyond your wildest imagination, you still have only so much time on this earth and so many hours before you need to sleep.

Efficiency in a training context means making the best use of your resources to achieve the goal of competency in defensive shooting skill. Remember the states of expectation? In order to make the most efficient use of your training resources, you need to determine what you're preparing for, because no one has unlimited amounts of time, energy, or money to prepare for everything that's merely possible. You need to prioritize your training for the kinds of threats you will plausibly face. You need to understand what you're preparing for and choose the appropriate skills to train (remember context?).

In addition, you need to learn and practice those skills in the most efficient manner possible. Curriculum or practice routines which have you do things that aren't appropriate to your self-defense goals waste your training resources. They are inefficient.

Efficiency in response

If you're forced to use your snubnose revolver against a real attacker, you'll be using your defensive resources: time (in very short increments), energy (your physical strength and stamina), ammunition (if the correct response is shooting), and sometimes space (you may not have the room or proximity you need to do certain things). Your overriding goal is to reliably stop the attacker from hurting you (or other innocents) by making the best use of those resources. The actual techniques you learn and use should respect that your defensive resources are limited.

Faster doesn't necessarily mean more efficient
Many people make the mistake of using "faster" to mean "more efficient." They're not the same!

Just because something is fast doesn't mean it's more efficient. Looking back at what efficiency means, it includes the goal (to do or produce something). In the case of self defense with a firearm, the goal is to make the attack stop in the most reliable manner possible. That goal is affected by everything in the environment:

- your mental and physical states as well as those of your attacker
- whether the environment is cold or hot, dry or wet
- if it's daylight or nighttime
- how many innocent people are around
- what you're standing on
- whether you were surprised or prepared
- if you have one hand or two to hold the snubby
- and much more

When you evaluate what's "efficient," you have to factor in the goal and the environment in which it happens. Let's take reloading the snubby as an example: If you always practice that reload for ideal conditions (i.e., you're standing still on a clean, warm, dry, and nicely lit range) and you're suddenly thrust into an incident at night, in the rain, and you're moving to avoid the guy with the knife, you might find yourself fumbling the reload. A reloading method that might be slightly slower in an absolute sense but is more easily accomplished under the worst plausible conditions is more efficient, because it takes into account the conditions under which it is being used.

Context and efficiency

This idea of making the best use of your resources is dependent upon the context of the skill — where it originates — particularly when how you'll be using it is different from where it originated. In the section on Context, I also used the example of reloading the snubby: in a competition, speed is the overriding goal (shoot faster than the other competitors). A technique that makes one shooter faster than the other shooters is efficient because of the pure nature of the goal.

As we've discussed, in a defensive shooting context, the overriding goal is to survive the encounter by making the attack stop as reliably as possible. This means that resistance to, and applicability over, a wide range of environmental conditions are probably more important than sheer speed under ideal conditions. Faster, therefore, is not always more efficient in this specific context. Speed (use of time) is only one thing you need to consider.

What about effectiveness?

Efficiency takes effectiveness into consideration. Since efficiency in a self-defense context always has the goal of stopping the attack as reliably as possible, techniques that help you do so while making the best use of resources are efficient by definition. But not all things that are effective are efficient!

For instance, simply firing lots of rounds blindly into the air may cause your attacker to give up out of sheer panic (don't laugh, it's happened more than once). This kind of "cover fire" might be effective in some cases, but it's a waste of ammunition as well as the time and effort required to shoot it, because it's not the most reliable way to stop an attack.

Firing rapid, multiple, accurate rounds into the center of the attacker's chest will also cause him to give up, but takes less time, effort, and ammunition to reliably achieve the goal. Hitting the target accurately and quickly will be effective more often than rounds fired into the air, and is efficient because it makes good use of defensive resources. In other words, if your focus in training is always on efficiency, effectiveness will be the inevitable by-product. Do not confuse these terms!

All the techniques you'll learn in this book are efficient as a base condition: using the least of your limited defensive resources to achieve the goal of reliably stopping the attacker under the widest range of plausible circumstances.

COUNTER-AMBUSH METHODOLOGY

A common statement from victims of violence, regardless of their training, is that their attack was a surprise to them. They did not see the attack coming until it was already underway. That's because the ambush is the best way for a criminal to act!

If you think about it, any rational (or even semi-rational) criminal is going to spring his attack when he has the most advantage. That advantage occurs at the time his victim least expects the attack, even if that time lasts only a few moments. It maximizes his chances of success and minimizes his risks.* That's the reality of the criminal attack.

A defensive training model that assumes — as most do — any amount of readiness on your part is therefore by definition not reality-based. The things we do, and the skills we're able to use, when we're prepared ahead of time are different than when we're caught off guard and are forced to respond reactively rather than proactively. The method of responding to the surprise attack, and the way in which we train to do so, are referred to as counter-ambush methodology.**

How criminal attacks happen

The typical criminal assault very often involves deception or concealment to prevent the victim from recognizing that an attack is imminent (or in progress) until it's too late. This makes the attack much more difficult to defend against, tilting the odds firmly in favor of the attacker.

Now look at how most defensive shooting is usually taught. A disturbingly large percentage of instruction is based on target or competition shooting (remember context?), where the shooter knows ahead of time what needs to be shot, where it needs to be shot, and can predict the conditions under which the shooting will take place. It's calm, pleasant, and — except for a little performance anxiety — decidedly non-threatening.

But when reality intrudes, and those students are faced with real threats to their lives, they don't have time to get into just the "right" shooting stance. Their body's natural threat reactions drastically alter how they see, breathe, move, and even think. What happens? Most likely, their body improvises a response that does work well with what it's doing at the time. Since it's an untrained response, it's likely to be less efficient and less effective than one that has been practiced ahead of time.

That's where counter-ambush methodology shines. It takes the ways in which attacks happen — by surprise — into account, and factors in how the body is likely to react to a lethal surprise threat. The techniques that come out of counter-ambush methodology, and the way they're taught, develop your ability to respond efficiently to the attack you didn't know was coming. The skills you learn work with your body's natural threat reactions and reflect the "worst case" of being caught off guard.

Backwards compatible?

According to data of actual defensive shootings gathered by Tom Givens, a nationally recognized defensive shooting instructor, most attacks are in fact a surprise to the victim. Not all attacks are alike, however, and it's plausible that you might have advanced awareness of the need to use lethal force in the form of your snubnose revolver. Will those counter-ambush skills still be valid?

The short answer is yes! An important part of the counter-ambush approach to defensive shooting is that the skills that work in the worst case (when you've been surprised by the attack) also work in those instances where you have some advance notice. But the reverse is not always true: techniques based on being ready or having the time to plan an elaborate defense usually don't work too well when time is compressed and your body is in full alarm reaction to the threat.

Counter-ambush methodology is based on recognizing the attack as early as possible, recalling the skills appropriate to defeating the attacker, and then responding by performing those skills.

* — *Not everyone is rational, and some attacks happen without regard to the risk of capture. Being intoxicated or under the influence of drugs can affect a person's rationality. In most of the cases I've studied, however, the criminal has picked a time and a victim specifically because of the likelihood of success. Whether he's rational or not, the threat is the same and your response is likely to be the same.*

** — *The term "Counter Ambush Methodology" comes from the Combat Focus Shooting course from I.C.E. Training. Its author, Rob Pincus, has done a superb job of codifying what defensive shooting incidents in the private sector look like, as well as how to train and respond to them.*

MAKING DECISIONS

I review a lot of defensive shooting incidents as part of evaluating what does and doesn't work. When I look at defensive gun uses where there was a negative outcome — incidents that did not turn out to the defender's benefit — the failure is rarely due to a lack of shooting skill. Most of the time the failures are due to improperly identifying the target or, worse yet, incorrectly judging if lethal force was even warranted.

Anytime you encounter the possibility of the need for lethal force, the environment is liable to be chaotic and unpredictable; therefore, developing the ability to make judgements based on what your eyes and ears are telling you is critical.

The real problem in defensive training is that it's very difficult to recreate the kind of environment under which you might need to use a gun to defend yourself. It's not enough to frighten you during training! Ideally, a training environment would result in activating a true physiological fear response at some level. It can be done, but it's expensive and requires very specific and hard-to-find resources. The value of that kind of training also diminishes rapidly with repetition. As a result, very few people ever get the benefit of being able to participate in it.

But what we can do is recreate the need to evaluate the information your eyes and ears are gathering and the confusion it causes. This can be accomplished easily and cheaply at even the beginning levels. The information you process won't be the same as what you encounter in a real incident, of course, and the environment won't match, but the important parts of information processing and the decisions made based on what you find from that processing can be.

In the training environment, this is accomplished by forcing you to think about what you're doing, rather than reflexively pulling the trigger in response to a fixed stimulus. Several of the exercises presented in this book are designed to force you to gather information, quickly analyze it, and act on the result you find. That is the basis of evaluating information during an actual attack.

CONSOLIDATING YOUR SKILLS

As discussed in the section on Efficiency, your training resources are always limited. While defensive shooting skills aren't as complicated as some want to make them appear, they're still physical (and mental) skills that must be developed, and quite a few pieces are needed to make everything work correctly.

The question is: how many discrete skills and physical manipulations are there, and how many are really important to your training and defensive goals? Can you consolidate them without affecting your safety or preparedness?

Yes, you can! Being able to "re-purpose" skills and techniques, or picking skills that are applicable under a wider range of circumstances, reduces the number of things you have to learn. The fewer things you need to learn, the less time, effort, and money you'll spend learning them. How can you make this happen?

By doing as many things in the same way as you can.

Consistency is efficient

It's not glaringly obvious, but one of the things I focus on in the following chapters is consistency, which simply means doing things in the same way to the greatest degree possible.

For instance, one of the first exercises is Extend-Touch-Fire. You start with your snubnose revolver at the ready position and extend out to fire a shot. It's a simple movement. When you're later exposed to the process of drawing the snubby from the holster, the extension part of the drawstroke (and everything that follows) is the same as it was when shooting from the ready position during the Extend-Touch-Fire exercise. That consistency means you don't have to learn an entirely new skill set when you start drawing the snubby — you'll simply be building on what you've already learned and practiced.

The ready position itself is a study in consistency: the ready position puts the gun in roughly the same place you'll learn to reload the gun, which is where your strength and dexterity are at their greatest. It's also useful over a wide range of defensive environments, which means you don't have to learn a "special" ready position for each little variable in your environment.

While consistency is not the be-all, end-all of training, it's worth pursuing whenever it makes sense. I hope you'll find the information and techniques presented in this book are as consistent as possible!

ACCURACY AND PRECISION

"Precision" and "accuracy" are two different terms (concepts, really) that are often confused for each other. Understanding the difference is important to your skill development!

Precision

Lots of people say "accuracy" when they really mean precision. Precision refers to the area of the target in which the shots need to be placed. In a training course, that area is the defined space on the target where every shot is worth exactly the same amount as every other shot. If your bullets hit within that area, and there is no smaller area delineated, you have been as precise as the target requires you to be.

Of course, in a defensive situation, your attacker doesn't give you the courtesy of having that area of precision spray-painted on his shirt! When applied to defensive shooting, precision refers to the area in which each shot will contribute the maximum amount to stopping the attack. You need to apply your skill (control over your snubnose revolver) to cause your rounds to land inside that area.

Precision is recognized

In both cases, the target dictates the precision you need to deliver. It's your job to understand the level of precision the target dictates, and then apply the level of skill necessary to put your bullets there. Precision, therefore, is recognized: you look at the target and determine how much skill you need to use to hit inside the level of precision it dictates.

Learning to recognize the level of precision needed is a skill that shows up in many of the exercises later in the book.

Accuracy

Accuracy, on the other hand, refers to whether or not any given shot actually hits within the area of precision you've recognized. Accuracy is a digital concept; it is "yes" or "no." You either hit within the area of precision or you didn't. If your shot hits within the area of precision, it is accurate; if it hits outside that area, it is not accurate. Either you delivered the precision needed or you didn't.

Because accuracy means shooting to the required level of precision (as dictated by the target), there can be no such thing as "more accurate" or "less accurate." Shooting smaller groups means shooting to a greater degree of precision, but accuracy always refers to whether it was achieved.

Since you don't get to choose the area of precision, your job is to apply your skill to put the bullets into the area the target has dictated. The measurement of your success is whether you were able to.

Efficiency

Can you choose to shoot to a greater level of precision than the target dictates? Certainly, and in fact a lot of training asks students to do just that: shoot smaller and smaller groups inside of the target area. When you analyze it, though, that's not efficient.

Think of it this way: if every bullet that hits into the area of precision is equal to every other one, spending more of your time and using more of your energy to shoot to an artificially higher level of precision gains you nothing for the expenditure. If you're choosing to do something that uses more resources when you could use fewer to get the same result (achieve the same goal), what you've chosen is less efficient.

If you're shooting at the center of your attacker's chest and your shots are all hitting accurately inside that area, all your rounds are contributing their statistical maximum to causing his incapacitation. If you take the time and expend the energy to cluster your rounds closer together, none of those bullets is likely to be doing a better job than the others — but your use of resources means you'll be able to shoot fewer of them in any given amount of time.

Since the data we have suggests that shooting more rounds accurately achieves faster and more reliable incapacitation, wouldn't it be better to shoot faster and accept a little less artificial precision? I think it is!

At the same time, inaccurate shots are also less efficient. If your rounds land outside the area of precision they may damage your attacker, but they don't do as much to bring about his incapacitation as the shots that land inside the target area. They also waste some of your resources. You're better off applying enough skill to bring those shots into the area of precision you've recognized so they'll help stop the attack more reliably.

Remember the section where we talked about *Processing Information?* Here's where it starts to become important: if you don't *recognize* the level of precision the target requires, you won't apply the level of skill to deliver it, and your rounds won't have the maximum effect. Shots that don't contribute their maximum to stopping your attacker waste a small amount of your time, energy, and available ammunition — they are inefficient. Being able to recognize the level of precision, then delivering it, is being efficient!

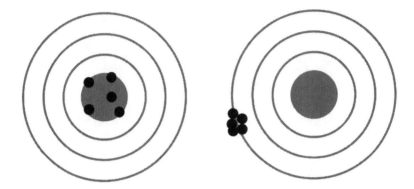

Target on left is accurate but not particularly precise; target on right is very precise, but not accurate.

BALANCE OF SPEED AND PRECISION

The more skill you apply to hit the area of precision, the more time it takes you to fire each round. It's less efficient to apply more skill than you need — to shoot to a higher level of precision than you need to — than to apply just the right amount of skill to get the maximum number of shots into the area where they can do you the most good. All of that in the least amount of time!

This idea is more easily referred to as the *Balance of Speed and Precision*, which is the core of what you'll be learning and practicing in the exercises later in this book. If you've been shooting for any length of time, you've been making use of that balance without really thinking about it. When faced with a "tougher" shot, you've probably buckled down, been more careful, and accepted that you were going to spend more time making the shot. That's the balance of speed and precision in action!

All shooting, including defensive shooting, is a balance of speed and precision. At its simplest, it means that an increase in precision needs a corresponding increase in your application of skill, and that results in a decrease in speed. On the other hand, an increase in speed usually results in a decrease in precision. There's more to it, but that relationship is the key.

This isn't a new concept, either. If you've been shooting much at all, you already have an intuitive grasp of the concept. It's been written about for years. The earliest book I have talks about the concept (though erroneously using accuracy instead of the more correct precision) way back in 1953! It's not something I made up for this book,* and it isn't just for target shooting.

Your balance of speed and precision will change with a host of variables, and your balance in any given situation will be different than someone else's in the same situation. Your own balance will change from day to day, and will even change over the length of a training or practice session as your fatigue level increases. Knowing your balance over a wide range of these variables is the reason for frequent practice!

The target dictates precision

As pointed out in the section about Accuracy and Precision, your target dictates the precision needed. Remember that on a paper target, the precision is dictated by the markings, but in a defensive shooting, that area is one you need to figure out — and quickly! Your attacker's physiology and position relative to you dictate the precision needed, but intervening obstacles — such as other people or things he's hiding behind or that are between you and him —factor into that area as well. In all cases, it falls to you to recognize the precision needed and apply the amount of your skill necessary to deliver that level of precision.

Skill determines accuracy

On the other hand, it's your skill — or more precisely, your application of your skill — that causes your shots to land inside the target area. Your application of your skill, therefore, determines whether you're accurate (or not.) You'll likely always experience some deviation between where you intend the shot to go and where it actually does, and controlling that deviation is how accuracy is achieved. Controlling deviation means applying skill: control over the gun.

Of course, controlling deviation takes both time and effort on your part. A large target area very close to you requires less deviation control than a smaller target that is farther away. As more precision is needed, you need to apply more deviation control, which takes more time.

Back to recognition: you need to practice to associate a given level of deviation control with what the target is dictating, then recall how much deviation control you need to apply (and how to apply it). When you've done that, you actually apply your skill to make the shot.

It's not as complicated as it seems, and the exercises in this book — done properly and frequently — help you make those recognition and recall links without your even realizing it's happening!

Confidence in skill determines speed

Your confidence in your own abilities is a big part of this too, and determines how fast you'll choose to shoot (unless you're shooting out of panic).

Confidence is the correlation between what you think you can do and what you really can do. Confidence comes from your training and frequent practice, which is why training and practicing under realistic conditions (recognizing and delivering varying levels of precision) are so important.

If you're over-confident — you think you have more skill than you do — you'll probably shoot too quickly. Shooting faster than your skill level allows is a large part of why inaccuracy happens, and as we've discussed, inaccuracy is inefficient.

On the other hand, if you're under-confident — you don't believe in your own skills or you haven't practiced enough to really know what your skills are — you'll likely shoot with more control than is needed under the circumstances and as a result shoot much more slowly than you need to. Shooting more slowly is inefficient as well. It wastes time and may result in giving your attacker more time to hurt you before he's incapacitated.

Shooting too quickly or too slowly are both inefficient uses of your defensive resources. If your skills and your confidence in those skills are correctly linked, you'll always shoot as fast as you believe you can get accurate hits. You'll apply the correct amount of control over your gun (skill in deviation control) to get the hits you need, and actually get them!

* — *While not new, the modern codification of the Balance of Speed and Precision, and the exercise of the same name presented later, is relatively recent and comes courtesy of the Combat Focus Shooting program.*

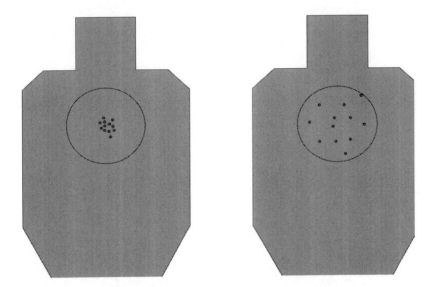

Shooting to a greater degree of precision than the target requires, as on the left, takes more effort and application of skill — which takes more time. Target on right shows an understanding of the balance of speed and precision: applying enough control to shoot to the level of skills the target requires, but no more.

NATURAL THREAT REACTIONS

When you're surprised and attacked — when your mind has determined you are facing a lethal threat — your body goes through a number of reactions, physiological changes, in order to survive. In the world of self defense, this is as close to a certainty as we have because we've evolved these natural survival reactions to keep us alive.

While there are scores of minor reactions (because the body does a lot of things to prepare itself to survive) and a bit of variance in the details depending on just what the threat is, these are the major reactions that will affect your training.

Posture and orientation

Someone watching as you are attacked would see a definite change in your posture and orientation. When attacked, the human body prepares to defend itself — sometimes by running, sometimes by fighting. In either case, it prepares for action.

What you'll likely experience is your body going into a slight crouch, with your upper body leaning forward. This puts you into an ideal position to move, whether to run or pivot as your attacker moves. Your legs become springboards of a sort, balancing your weight yet allowing you to shift direction rapidly as you need to.

At the same time your posture is changing, so is your orientation: you're likely to turn your body toward and face your threat. This puts you into the most advantageous position in which to fight, while at the same time orienting your eyes so they can gather as much information as possible. Your mind wants to know what it's facing so it can make the kind of rapid decision necessary to insure your survival, and the only way to do that is to look at the threat directly. The best way to look at the threat directly is if you're facing it head-on, which is what I mean by "orientation."

As you drop into that very athletic stance, your hands are likely to be moving as well. This can be seen in many surveillance videos of surprise attacks: the hands move rapidly and convulsively toward the head in an instinctive move to protect the brain and visual systems. If the threat stimulus is audible, like a blast or gun shot, the hands tend to cover the head. If it's visual, like someone swinging a club at you, they tend to come up in front of the face to prevent contact. In either event, your hands are not likely to be hanging passively at your side!

Vision and fixation

What an onlooker sees is not what you'll see, and that's because part of the natural threat reaction is a significant change in your vision. You've heard of "tunnel vision" when people are threatened? That's just the most obvious manifestation of a complex and remarkable reaction!

Your eyes have a split blood supply: one part supplies the majority of the muscles and sensors in your retina, while another separate source supplies the fovea centralis: the small part of your retina that contains most of the high-resolution, color-sensitive cone cells your eye uses to resolve fine detail. (The fovea is a tiny area — only 1.5mm in diameter — yet uses up half of the optical nerves going to the brain!)

When your brain has sensed you are under a dangerous threat, the blood supply to the majority of the eye diminishes and that of the fovea increases. This results in a huge increase in visual acuity in the middle of your field of vision, and a substantial reduction in the amount of information coming from the rest of the retina. This is why tunnel vision happens: Your brain is focusing more on the great amount of information your fovea is sending, and less on the smaller amount of data from the rest of your retina.

As that blood supply is reduced, your pupils dilate. This is a benefit to the cones in the fovea, which need a lot of light to function, but it also reduces your depth perception. The diminished blood flow also affects the muscles that control focusing, causing their functioning to slow. The result is that your physical focus tends to become fixed on your threat.

In addition to your visual fixation on the threat, you're likely to experience a profound psychological fixation. Your brain devotes everything it has to one job: defeating the threat in front of it. Everything else becomes secondary, allowing you to center your attention on what you need to do to save your life.

Strength and dexterity

Changes in blood flow aren't limited to your eyes. Your body also reduces blood flow to the small capillaries in your extremities in favor of major muscle groups. This may have evolved to stem blood loss in the vulnerable hands and feet: the less blood that's flowing through them, the less bleeding will occur when they're injured. Remember the movement of the hands to protect the head? Putting them in the line of attack means they're more likely to be injured, and keeping those injuries from resulting in major blood loss would seem to be a big survival positive.

But when dealing with defensive tools like the snubnose revolver, that reduction in blood flow means you'll experience a reduction in both strength and dexterity in your hands. You may also seem to shake uncontrollably, which is a combination of the hormones being released into your system and the reduced muscle control because of the change in blood flow.

Natural threat reactions can't be trained away

The important thing to remember is that these are natural reactions over which you have no control. Once your amygdala — the small part of your brain that pattern matches incoming sensory information and helps you to recognize danger — has initiated your physical fear reactions, they're going to work the way they do. Those physical reactions can't be trained away and so must be accounted for in your training. However, your amygdala can, with repeated exposure, become accustomed to certain stimuli and not respond as aggressively.*

When you're attacked, when you're surprised by a predatory criminal, your body is likely to do the things it's evolved to do to survive. The question is: How will you deal with those changes?

How natural threat reactions affect your training

It's my firm belief that the best things you can do are take advantage of your body's natural threat reactions and use their survival positives the way they were intended. This means training in ways that work with your body's reactions rather than working against them — or worse, pretending you don't need to be concerned with them!

As a result, the techniques that follow are all chosen and developed to work with your natural reactions. For instance, instead of suggesting a contrived shooting stance, I have you shooting from a posture that's similar to what your body does when it's surprised by an attack. Instead of techniques that require a great amount of dexterity, I have you reduce your reliance on fine motor skills to the greatest degree possible. Instead of pretending you'll have the same perfect vision you have on the range when practicing, you'll learn how to aim your snubby even when you can't expect to focus on your sights.

Working with your built-in survival traits, rather than working against them, allows you to respond more efficiently when it really matters!

— http://www.dana.org/Publications/Brainwork/Details.aspx?id=43615

READY POSITION

You hear a lot about "ready positions" in the shooting world. A ready position is simply where and how your snubby is held when it's in your hands, ready to shoot, but isn't yet being shot. It's an administrative position; a parking space where it's safe, can't be easily taken, but can be immediately employed — or put back into the holster. The ready position can also be thought of as a "home" or "rest" position, a place where it can be held for periods of time without tiring you out.

Everyone, it seems, has their favorite ready position, and some people advocate different ready positions for different purposes. But in the context of defensive shooting in the private sector, the ideal ready position should do several things to help you do your job of protecting yourself:

- It should allow you to extend into your shooting position in a way that's consistent with how the snubby comes out of the holster.
- It should give you maximum control of your snubnose in the event your attacker tries to take it away.
- It should make it easy and safe to move with the snubby in your hands.
- To the greatest degree possible, it should be consistent with where the snubby will be when reloading and performing administrative functions.

My preferred ready position

The one position I've found that encompasses all those desired traits is variously referred to as the "chest ready" or "high compressed ready" (and there are probably other names for it.) In this book, I'm simply going to call it the "ready position." This ready position delivers on all the criteria I mentioned above: it's consistent with all the tasks you may need to do, such as reloading; it's the position where your strength and dexterity are greatest; it's a protected position, which allows efficient movement when necessary; and it's also comfortable to hold for moderate periods of time!

Mechanics of the ready position

Hold your snubby with muzzle pointed downrange (at the target) with the barrel roughly parallel to the ground. It's okay for the muzzle to point slightly downward, but the barrel shouldn't tilt up. In most cases, especially at a shooting range, pointing at the sky to any degree is not a generally safe direction.

Your hands (and gun) should end up roughly around the base of your sternum (that little "pit" at the bottom of your ribcage). I say "roughly" because individual physiology determines where it is most comfortable for you. Your elbows should be tucked into the sides of your torso — again, comfortably as opposed to exaggerated.

If you remember the section on Consistency, this ready position is consistent with how you'll learn to draw your snubby from the holster. The resulting position, in front of the chest, is similar to where the hands usually meet during the draw from the holster. It's also where reloading the snubnose revolver can be done most efficiently.

If you consider the risk of an assailant trying to take your weapon from you (it happens), this ready position is where your arms and upper body are at their strongest, allowing you to resist a "gun grab" from most angles.

Finally, it's a position that permits easy and efficient movement around obstacles or through doorways. If you point the muzzle strongly downward (but not at your feet!), moving around other people with snubby in hand becomes safer for everyone involved.

The ready position in practice

Make the ready position a comfortable part of your gun handling, and this goes not just for your snubnose but for any handgun you shoot. Discipline yourself to come to the ready position whenever you're getting ready to shoot, even if just plinking. When you finish a string of shots, instead of dropping the gun down, as most people tend to do, come back to the ready position. It should be the "last stop" before holstering the snubnose.

You'll probably spend more time in the ready position than actually shooting. Get comfortable with it!

Proper ready position: gun in as close as is comfortable, elbows to the sides

GRASP

Grasp refers to the way your hands contact and hold the snubnose revolver when you're shooting. Some people use the term "grip" instead, but that can get confusing because the term is also often used to refer to the parts of the gun the hands contact! It can end up sounding a little like this: "Grip the snubby with a solid grip on the grips." Confusing? I think so too, and that's why I use the term grasp in this book and in my classes.

A good grasp is the first fundamental of shooting, particularly with the snubnose revolver. You need to control the snubby's recoil during rapid multiple shots, when the recoil of the rounds being fired has a tendency to flip the revolver up and backward.

What is muzzle flip and why does it happen?
This "muzzle flip" is due to the pivot point (the uppermost point of your hand's contact) being below the axis of the bore. The farther the bore gets from that pivot point (the higher above your hands), the more apparent recoil you'll feel and the more the muzzle will jump when the gun is fired.

Imagine holding a stick in your fist. If someone pushed the stick right where it exits your fist, they'd need to use a lot of force to get the stick to move. If they apply the same force at the end of the stick, away from your hand, the stick moves much farther with less effort. The same happens with your snubnose!

An efficient grasp minimizes felt recoil by getting your hands as high up on the gun — as close to the bore line — as possible, while still allowing you to reach and operate the trigger.

Proper snubnose grasp

One of the reasons autoloading pistols seem to have lower recoil is due to their tang or "beavertail." That little appendage helps stabilize the gun's rearward flip against the muscles between your thumb and forefinger, and it works pretty well in keeping the gun from both flipping and sliding down inside your fist.

Because the snubnose revolver doesn't have that tang, your shooting hand has to do a different job in controlling recoil. You need to keep the gun from moving in your hands through proper grasp rather than relying on an autoloader's beavertail. If you're coming to the snubby from a pistol, you'll notice that your grasp needs to be different and requires more muscle strength in your fingers.

One key to an efficient snubby grasp is to set up a constriction effect with the shooting hand to stop the gun from rotating down and out of your grasp. Here's how to do that:

1. Safety first: Make sure your trigger finger is on the frame underneath the cylinder, above the trigger!

2. Place your shooting hand as high on the backstrap of the snubby as possible, but not so high that the web between your thumb and forefinger flows over the shoulder of the frame. The shoulder is typically quite square and can transmit painful recoil forces into the web of your hand, which is why you place the web as high as you can without covering that shoulder.

3. Once you have the web of the shooting hand properly positioned, wrap your fingers around the grip. Your fingers should, as much as possible, stay in contact with each other. Look at the side of the grips: there should be a gap between the tips of the fingers and the heel of the hand. The smaller the snubby and/or the bigger your hands, the less gap there may be.

4. Curl your shooting thumb strongly downward, toward your middle finger. You should feel a natural constriction between your thumb and middle finger. This constriction is a big part of recoil control on the snubnose revolver.

5. If you're shooting with two hands (and under most circumstances, you should be), the heel of your support hand should go into the gap between the fingers and palm. If in your case there is no gap, put the heel of the support

hand on the nails of the shooting hand's fingers. Your support hand's thumb is curled down so its pad firmly contacts the thumbnail of the shooting hand.*

The resulting grasp should have a strong constriction effect between the thumb and forefinger of the shooting hand, which the support hand reinforces. This keeps the revolver from sliding down in the grasp during recoil.

Pay attention to grasp pressure!

Where and how your hands are placed are important, but just as important is how hard you grasp the gun. The amount of pressure or "squeeze" you apply to your snubby is vital to controlling recoil. Because the snubnose typically recoils more than a full-sized revolver (let alone an autoloading pistol), you need to apply more control — more grasp pressure — in order to keep the gun stable during recoil.

Your grasp pressure is important in another way: It's how you keep the snubby from moving off target as you depress the trigger. In fact, I consider proper grasp and sufficient grasp pressure to be the most important components in accurate double-action shooting!

How much grasp pressure any one person can exert is of course highly individualized and dependent on hand strength, but you should always exert the maximum amount of grasp pressure possible without causing the muscles of your arms and hands to tremble. The next section includes an exercise that will help you determine what your own maximum pressure is. That pressure should be applied every time the gun is extended to shoot.

Grasp pressure should be equalized among all the fingers and between both hands. One hand applying a different amount of pressure than the other causes no end of training difficulties and makes recoil control unpredictable.

Pay particular attention to the fingers of the shooting hand. Each one should contribute pressure on the gun's grips. It's common for shooters to apply lots of pressure with the stronger thumb and middle finger and ignore the ring and pinky fingers. Without sufficient "squeeze" at the bottom of the grip by those two fingers, it's almost impossible to achieve good recoil control.

I admit it's a lot to think about! As I said at the top, the grasp is the most important contributor to being able to deliver the rapid, multiple, accurate shots you'll need against an attacker. It's worth devoting the time to master it.

* — *Alternative support-hand thumb position: If you have a small revolver and large hands, you may find that your support-hand thumb interferes with your trigger finger's movement. If that's your problem, you can curl the support-hand thumb on top of the first knuckle of the shooting-hand thumb, rather than on top of the shooting-hand thumbnail. This should keep the support-hand thumb well clear of the trigger finger and allow you to manipulate the trigger unimpeded. (However, under no circumstances should the support thumb be wrapped around the back of the shooting hand as you see in the movies! This always results in a reduction in recoil control and sets up a habit that can be dangerous should you also shoot a semiautomatic pistol. Don't do it!)*

Firing hand gets good, high grasp on the gun; note gap between fingers and palm

Heel of support hand is placed into gap...

...and support fingers are wrapped around, with thumbs curled down.

STANCE

Far too much ink has been spilled debating shooting stances without a clear understanding of what a stance is or needs to be in a defensive encounter.

As I mentioned in the section on Natural Threat Reactions, when you're faced with a lethal threat your body is likely to respond in very specific ways. One of those regards your physical orientation to the threat: slightly crouched, knees flexed, body leaning aggressively forward. That's how the human animal prepares to fight — or to defend itself.

How you train to use a handgun to defend yourself should take advantage of that natural threat response posture. By doing so, you'll be training and practicing in a way that your body understands intuitively, which makes it easier to execute under a threat response.

Looking at the shooting stance

Your shooting stance has two separate components, which can be easily divided into Below The Waist (BTW) and Above The Waist (ATW).

In general, what happens below the waist is more affected by environmental variables and is less important to your ability to control your snubby. Above the waist is another matter: You want to control what happens there because it's more important to your response and your ability to shoot well. Pay more attention to what happens above the waist than below.

Below the waist

When I talk about the Below The Waist portion of the stance, I'm primarily talking about your feet. It's important to understand that foot positioning is a training convenience and nothing more. This is because, in a defensive shooting incident, that part of your stance is going to be unpredictable. The surface on which you're standing, the direction you're facing when an imminent attack is recognized, and many other factors will all contribute to exactly what that part of your stance looks like. If you have one foot on the sidewalk and one on the pavement when you're faced with an attacker, your feet might stay in exactly that position, but they might also move. In either case, you need to be able to shoot well regardless of where your feet end up!

Because your actual defensive stance is unpredictable, it's best to practice from an adaptable position. I suggest adopting a neutral, natural athletic stance for your training and practice. This allows you to learn defensive shooting skills without bias to any particular positioning, and later you can adapt and practice shooting from less ideal positions (and in fact, that's exactly what you should do!)

The natural, neutral stance lets you more quickly and easily adapt to "off balance" conditions, the kind under which you might actually end up shooting. If you adopt an exaggerated stance for your practice, one that is intentionally biased in some direction, when you actually encounter a situation that is the polar opposite of that stance, you'll find it much harder to adapt than if you always practiced at the mid-point between them. The degree of change is less in the neutral position.

Natural, neutral

What does this natural, neutral stance look like? Stand with your feet roughly parallel to the target and about shoulder-width apart. This reflects your body's natural tendency to square off to a threat and adopt a position where it can move quickly and easily in any direction. Your knees should be slightly bent (or "unlocked") to help lower your body's center of gravity. This allows you both stability and rapid movement — again, part of what your natural threat reactions will seek. Your hips, like your feet, should be roughly parallel to the threat/target.

Don't worry about exactly where your feet end up. That's really not important. As long as they're not in an exaggerated position (one foot noticeably behind the other) and are roughly parallel to the target, that's enough. What you want to avoid is a foot position where you look like you're on a skateboard or snowboard: one foot dramatically behind the other and the line between them more perpendicular, rather than parallel, to the target.

Above the waist

This is where you need to devote most of your stance-related attention. Your upper body should lean forward from the hips, as if you are slightly bowing to someone. This forces the buttocks backward to help balance your body's weight over your feet. Combined with your slightly bent knees, this lean should resemble a slight crouch.

Square off your shoulders to the threat/target. While you shouldn't worry about whether your feet or hips are exactly squared off, make sure your shoulders are. This is consistent with your body's natural desire to face the threat and prepare to fight. It also lets your arms properly extend into a shooting position.

Speaking of your arms, they should be extended equally and straight out from your body as far as is comfortably possible. Some people aren't able to extend their arms to the point that the elbows lock into their stiff-arm position. Your individual skeletal and muscular make-up determines whether you can. If you have a lot of muscle around your upper torso, for instance, you may not be able to achieve that amount of extension.

The goal is always the maximum amount of extension possible, because your body's natural reaction is likely to thrust your snubby out as far as possible. Since that's what your body does naturally, the intuitive way to train is to do the same thing!

When you've extended the snubnose out as far as you can, it should be on the centerline of your body. This puts it into your line of sight, where evolution has taught humans to use tools most efficiently. (Again, when you are surprised by a lethal threat, you're likely to use tools the way you've evolved to do so: in the center of your field of vision.)

As you reach full extension, your shoulders should be rolled forward. This engages the muscles of your back and upper arms to more easily control recoil by channeling it into your skeletal system.

Viewed from above, the result resembles a triangle with your head on the centerline. This stance gives solid recoil control, engagement of your visual system in the way it's used to working, and works with your body's natural threat reactions to make an efficient and intuitive response to a lethal threat.

Natural, neutral stance: knees flexed, bowing slightly from the waist, arms extended with shoulders rolled forward for recoil control

EXTENSION

Extension is the act of bringing the snubby from the ready position (or moving through the ready position as part of drawing the gun) into the shooting position. Doing it efficiently is one of the keys to being able to get rapid, multiple, accurate hits on target. Paying a bit of attention to the mechanics will help you make the extension faster, smoother, more consistent, and ultimately safer.

An efficient extension also makes getting an accurate first-round hit more certain. The first round you shoot is your best opportunity to affect your attacker's ability to present a lethal threat to you, so it should be accurate and happen as quickly as possible. A rapid yet solid extension makes that possible.

The extension is the same fundamental action whether it occurs from the ready position or as your snubnose is coming up out of the holster, and regardless of using one or both hands. In either case, the gun starts somewhere in front of your chest and is pushed forward toward the target, ending up in the centerline of your body (with both arms locked out) and the gun in your line of sight.

Mechanics of the extension

Whether you're starting from the ready position or drawing from the holster, as your snubby moves forward, it also has to come up into your line of sight. Imagine the movement of an escalator: simultaneously moving up and forward.

The important thing to remember is you want to get the snubby up into your line of sight as early as possible. Ideally, your gun should break into your line of sight roughly halfway through the extension. (Don't worry about that happening at some exact point. Somewhere around half is the goal.)

As the gun moves forward, it needs to also move rapidly up into your line of sight. Ideally, the last half of the extension should be straight out toward the target, with no more vertical movement. Should a shot need to be fired at any point along that line, your snubby will still be crudely indexed on target despite not being at full extension. Continuing the escalator analogy, the extension should look like riding the escalator up, then walking off the escalator straight into the housewares department!

Watch muzzle movement!
As you extend your snubby toward the target, take care that the muzzle stays indexed on target. In my classes, it's common to see both new and experienced shooters "bowling" (the muzzle dipping down and then being pulled back up) and "flycasting" (muzzle points up, then has to be brought down to the target). Both of those are wasted movements and reduce your ability to get that fast, accurate first round on target. Again, the escalator metaphor is useful: the barrel stays indexed on target and simply rises as it's going forward. The muzzle won't stay perfectly still, and that's not the intention, but it shouldn't dip up or down to any great degree.

Stance and grasp

As you're extending out to that shooting position, tighten your grasp to your own maximum. At the same time, your body should be assuming the natural threat reaction posture: forward lean, lowered center of gravity, knees slightly bent. Your arms should extend equally to keep your gun on your body's centerline, where your body is accustomed to using all manner of tools and where your visual system works best.

As your arms reach their full forward movement, if your physical make-up allows it, your elbows should "toggle over" or lock into position. Minimal muscle mass is required to maintain the locked-out position compared to a bent-arm position.* If you tighten your biceps when you reach full extension, it's easier to keep your arms firmly locked against the recoil of the gun.

Roll your shoulders forward, engaging the biceps (to lock the elbows) and the upper back muscles (to help make the torso more rigid). This helps dramatically with recoil control — especially for those of us who weren't blessed with large upper-body muscle mass!

When you reach the end of your extension, when your snubby is locked into alignment with the target, move your trigger finger from its position on the frame and into contact with the trigger. Depending on the circumstances of an actual attack, you might elect to bring the trigger finger to the trigger earlier, but while you're training, it's important to develop the discipline of trigger finger control by touching the trigger only when you're at full extension.

*— *Some people may not be able to extend their arms to the point that their elbows "toggle over." This might be due to injury, extra mass in the chest area (bodybuilders are particular examples of this), or joint issues such as arthritis or bursitis. If this describes you, just extend the gun forward to your physical limit and use the muscle mass of your arms to control the recoil. Consciously tightening the muscles of both your upper and lower arms to serve as "shock absorbers" for your snubby's recoil are likely to give you the best results.*

Start of the extension, from the ready position. Note elbows tucked into sides of body and forward lean.

Gun comes up into the line of sight at the same time it moves forward, much like an escalator.

Last one-third to one-half of the extension is straight out toward the target, finishing in a solid shooting stance.

TRIGGER CONTROL

Trigger control in a defensive context means not allowing the movement of the trigger finger to affect the alignment of the gun. Even with a solid grasp, poor trigger control can lead to pushing or "steering" the gun, throwing the muzzle off target and resulting in inaccurate shots. Your task is to deliver rapid, multiple, accurate shots on target in order to efficiently incapacitate your attacker, and good trigger control will help you do that.

Grasp Is the foundation of trigger control

Trigger control — manipulating the trigger in a way that doesn't throw the muzzle off target — is a vital aspect of shooting a snubnose revolver. The foundation of good trigger control is the grasp, and I encourage you to re-read the section on Grasp because without it good trigger control will be difficult if not impossible.

It's helpful to put this in perspective: the typical snubby, even a heavy steel model, weighs about 24 ounces. That's a pound-and-a-half. An aluminum or other lightweight alloy version can weigh less than half that! The trigger weight on those guns will, from the factory, be in the neighborhood of 10-12 pounds. Even in the best case, your trigger finger will apply pressure at a level of more than six-and-a-half times the weight of the gun (and could actually be double that!) The excess force has to be controlled, and the only way to do so is through a solid grasp.

No matter how well trained your trigger finger is, without a solid grasp, the gun will move as you move the trigger.

Trigger control needs to start with proper grasp, which includes a solid extension. The more physical control you can apply to your snubby, the easier it is to manipulate the trigger without steering the muzzle off your target. A solid grasp and extension make it much harder for your trigger finger to move the gun, no matter how quickly you shoot or how convulsively you operate the trigger.

That last point is important because, during a surprise lethal attack, your body's natural threat reactions are most likely to result in a reduction in tactile sensation in your extremities. The hard science says it's unlikely you're going to have a good feel for your finger against the trigger, and it's a pretty good bet your fine control over the muscles in your trigger finger will diminish. That combination can result in more-than-expected deviation of your muzzle as your trigger finger convulses on the trigger and twists the gun in your grasp. It's not a lot, but it doesn't take a lot to throw a shot off the point of aim!

The stronger your grasp and the more solid your extension, the more likely the positive effects of your body's natural reactions (strength in large muscle masses) will offset the lack of feeling and control in the smaller muscle groups of your fingers. This underscores why it makes sense to train in the way the body is likely to behave when threatened.

If you're pulling shots off target, particularly in rapid fire, first revisit your grasp and extension. Make sure they're both solid before worrying about trigger finger issues. If your grasp and extension are weak, it will be very difficult to modulate the muscles of your trigger finger enough to compensate.

Operating the trigger rapidly

Once the grasp and extension issues are sorted out, you can consider how you're manipulating the trigger. I've found some commonalities with trigger control issues, and it's likely that if you have an issue it will be due to one of these habits.

Many students try to "grab" at the trigger in a misguided attempt to get the shot to go off as quickly as possible. The sudden acceleration causes the muscles of the hand to pull the gun in one direction, while the sudden stop when the trigger reaches the bottom of its travel often steers the gun in the opposite direction.

The key in snubnose trigger control is to accelerate the trigger finger rapidly but smoothly. A useful analogy is using the accelerator in your car to merge into freeway traffic on a rainy day: Unless you're intentionally trying to spin your tires, you don't normally shove the accelerator to the floor as hard as you can! Instead, you smoothly but quickly press the accelerator as far as necessary so your car accelerates as quickly as possible while keeping the tires in contact with the pavement.

Keeping that analogy in mind helps to understand why you need to eliminate both the sudden start and sudden stop of the trigger. Rather than thinking about moving the trigger, think of your trigger finger as rapidly increasing the pressure on the trigger until the gun fires. Focusing on the increase in pressure, and modulating how quickly that pressure is applied depending on the circumstances, reduces the tendency toward the "hard acceleration" that plagues so many snubby owners.

Rolling the trigger straight back

Controlling how your finger applies pressure to the trigger is the first step, but controlling the direction that force is applied is equally important! If your finger applies force to the trigger in any direction other than parallel to the bore of the barrel, the muzzle can (and likely will) be steered off target, resulting in an inaccurate shot.

It's simple: the trigger needs to be rolled straight back, and I've found it's useful for my students to visualize the trigger — not their finger, but the trigger itself — coming back directly at their nose. In a normal, proper shooting stance, your nose should be directly behind the gun. If you think about the trigger traveling directly back at your nose, your finger is likely to apply pressure in exactly the right direction. This is a mental trick that helps your brain control the force of your trigger finger over a longer baseline than just the fraction of an inch the trigger will move. This isn't unlike golf or tennis — where "follow through" includes a large movement after the ball is hit, giving the club or racket a target well beyond what it has to hit.

Trigger finger positioning

Sometimes a major issue is just how the trigger finger is positioned on the face of the trigger. Finger placement can dramatically affect the direction the trigger is pushed and, in extreme cases, can't easily be compensated for even with the nose trick.

Ideally your finger contacts the trigger at, or just to the outside of, your finger's first (distal interphalangeal) joint. Too far to one side or the other and you'll be applying your trigger force well off the gun's centerline, causing the muzzle to deviate from its alignment on target. This happens commonly when your gun is too large for your hand, because the finger can't quite reach the trigger at the optimal point. In those cases (assuming you want to keep that gun), you need to pay much more attention to modulating the trigger finger to keep the trigger moving straight backward.

This isn't usually the case with most snubbies, as they tend to be built on small frames that fit a wider range of hand sizes. But of course it can happen! If you have very short fingers or your snubby has oversized grips, you might run into this fit issue. In that case, force ends up being applied to the side of the trigger because the finger can't easily push straight back.

I've also seen the opposite: the person with very large hands who has to contort to fit the small gun. That contortion makes it difficult to roll the trigger straight back. If this describes you, correcting the problem through technique is relatively easy. Big hands/small gun is a better problem to have than small hands/big gun!

Trigger finger manipulation

Even with perfect finger placement on the trigger, it's possible to steer the snubby off target. I often see the tip of the trigger finger curling toward the frame as the trigger comes back, which inevitably applies a side force to the gun and steers it off target. This can happen to anyone but is particularly common in people with strong or long fingers.

This is often as much a psychological issue as a physical one. Remember that the snubby's trigger doesn't come straight back: It travels in an arc as it pivots inside the frame, and moves upward at the same time it moves backward. Also at the same time, your trigger finger is moving in a complex curve because of the three pivot points (joints). The effect is something like a decreasing radius turn on a curvy road.

As the arcs of the trigger and your trigger finger interact, it's quite difficult to keep an absolutely constant point of contact. The trigger is moving one way and your finger another, and it feels like either your finger is going to slip off the trigger or the trigger is going to get away! The result is a tendency to try to "hang on" to the moving trigger. The tip of the trigger finger curls in to grab onto the trigger and keep the finger in a consistent place on the trigger face.

The best way I've found to counteract that tendency is to accept that the finger is going to move on the trigger. As the trigger moves back, your finger slides down the face of the trigger slightly, and moves in and out — across the trigger face — as that happens. It's a complex interaction to be sure, but the important point is to accept the movement. It's not a lot of movement, but you can feel it if you allow it to happen. Get comfortable with that feeling; just know that your finger isn't going to slip off the trigger, and the trigger isn't magically going to fall out of the frame. You don't need to hang onto it like a lifeline!

As gory as this may sound, imagine that the tip of your finger is missing and just the first joint is applying all the force to the face of the trigger. I'm not quite sure why that works, but many of my students tell me it's cured their tendency to curl the tip of their finger as they roll the trigger back.

Proper finger placement is important to good trigger control. Finger should contact trigger at or next to the first joint for best combination of control and leverage.

UNSIGHTED FIRE

The following may be the most controversial part of this book, but it really shouldn't be. Your visual system has evolved over the millennia to do some very specific things, but for some reason the defensive shooting world wants to pretend what science tells us about sight and vision can't possibly be true. The result has been an overemphasis on techniques that are not only unlikely to work when your body's natural threat reactions have been activated, but just aren't necessary in the first place.

Even a great competitive shooter like Rob Leatham knows this. In many interviews, he's stated that people usually miss because they're spending too much time worrying about aiming the gun. In reality, aiming a snubnose revolver, particularly at typical defensive distances, isn't difficult if you don't over-complicate things!

Your defensive shooting training should begin with unsighted fire, but don't be confused by the term. By "unsighted," I don't mean not using your eyesight, but rather not using the sights on the gun. Sights are not magical; they're simply fine alignment guides. It's possible, and in fact usually sufficient, to align your snubby on target without them. It's easy to do and congruent with how your eyesight works during your body's natural threat reactions, and the fastest way for you to get those rapid, multiple, accurate hits on a realistic target.

It all starts by doing something your body wants to do in the first place: look at the threat.

Threat fixation

If you recall the section on Natural Threat Reactions, one of them deals with changes to the blood supply in your eyes when you're under lethal attack.

Your eyes want to lock focus on your threat and your brain wants to allocate most of its attention on that threat. This is normal, it's natural, and it has kept humans alive when faced with all manner of predators. It's how we gather information about our threat and make decisions about how to respond; as legendary police shooting instructor Lou Chiodo says, "threat focus is necessary for threat awareness, which is necessary for good judgement."

The most efficient way to train, and the most intuitive way to learn skills, is to replicate to the greatest degree what your body does naturally when responding to an attack. In this case, you should train to utilize your eyesight like you will in a fight: by focusing on the threat.

In a training context, the more correct term for this is target focus. Instead of focusing on the gun, your eyes focus on the target. This is consistent (as are all the techniques in this book) with the way your body works when faced with a lethal threat. Focusing on the target works with those natural threat reactions instead of fighting them.

This doesn't mean you're going to shoot randomly or blindly. As it happens, the combination of physical alignment to the threat (orientation) and your line of sight to the target point is more than sufficient to align your snubby and make accurate hits out to surprising distances. How do you do this? Get squared off to the target (as covered in the section on Stance), and as you extend your snubby to the target, bring it INTO and PARALLEL WITH your line of sight. (Pay attention to the mechanics of how this happens by re-reading the section on Extension.)

In this method, your eyes are locked onto the point on the target/threat where you want your bullets to hit. This gives you a long and straight optical baseline, and your snubby is aligned on that baseline. To reiterate, you're not using the gun's sights. It's aligned on target through the combination of physical (proper extension and stance) and optical (target focus) cues.

In practice, just look at the point you need to hit and stay focused on that point as your snubnose is extended into your line of sight and the shot is fired. Most people — even absolute beginners — are surprised to find that this is sufficient to get rapid, multiple, accurate hits to an upper-chest-sized area at most plausible self-defense distances.* With practice, it's possible to get those same hits at implausible distances!

Retraining bad habits

Experienced shooters who've trained heavily in one of the many gun-focused shooting methods usually need to re-train themselves to focus on the threat instead of on their sights. I'm not usually a proponent of retraining established habits, because the benefit rarely exceeds the cost in training resources. This is one exception to my rule. I believe retraining in threat- or target-focused shooting techniques is important, because target focus is how the human body is likely to react to a sudden lethal threat. Target focus is an intuitive shooting skill, one that works well with what the body already does naturally.

On the other hand, training in techniques that work counter to how our bodies work may result in failure at a critical time. If your body is likely to have a threat fixation and a threat focus, and you haven't trained taking into account that reaction, how good are you going to be when the time comes? Again, you can't train away your body's natural reactions. You can choose to incorporate them into your training or not, but your body is unlikely to do something completely different than what it's evolved to do in the face of a lethal attack. I think retraining in target-focused shooting techniques is worth the effort, because it accustoms you to how you're likely to react when you're forced to fight.

Most of the criticism of threat- or target-focused shooting techniques I hear deals with the belief that you can't make accurate hits without precision alignment using the sights. On the contrary: most of my students discover that this target-focus technique allows them accurate shots on a realistic center-chest-sized area out to surprising distances. Since the best data we have* suggests that most (92%) defensive shootings in the private sector occur between three and seven yards, with the majority (84%) happening between just three and five yards, this technique proves to be more than sufficient to hit the area most likely to cause the attacker to stop. Each person's abilities are different, and learning what the limits of this natural technique are for you will happen with practice at varying distances.

Always fire multiple rounds (preferably a random number on each repetition of any exercise), but emphasize placing that all-important first round accurately inside the target area. Focus on the threat (target) before making the decision to shoot, and keep the focus on the target as the gun comes into and parallel with your line of sight and the shots are fired.

* — *Tom Givens/RangeMaster survey of student-involved shootings: www.american-handgunner.com/when-citizens-fight-back/*

USING THE SIGHTS

As touched on previously, there is nothing magic about sights. They're simply alignment guides that allow you to index your muzzle on target to a greater degree of precision than you can without them. But in the shooting world, they're treated with the kind of reverence normally reserved for religious icons. "Focus on the front sight" is a mantra that almost everyone has heard at some point in their shooting training, but as champion shooter Rob Leatham says, "I see more people screwing up ... because they're fixated on the front sight." *

Sights won't make up for not understanding the mechanics of shooting your snubby — namely, grasp and trigger control. It's faster, easier, and more intuitive to use the unsighted fire techniques in the last section. Using them also gives you accurate results with less effort.

When do you use your sights?

That's a trick question I use in most of my classes. When I ask students, "When should you use your sights?" I usually get the same answer: "Whenever you can."

That's the wrong answer! Regardless of whether you're in a training class or just practicing, you can always use your sights. When practicing, your vision hasn't been altered by your body's threat reactions. You're not trying to shoot a moving attacker and your attacker isn't swinging a baseball bat at your head. All those things — and several more — affect your ability to use your sights.

If "whenever you can" isn't the right answer, what is? When should you use your sights? It's simple: when your target dictates a greater level of precision. In other words, you use the sights on your snubby when you need to. You don't use them because you want to or because you can. You use them because you need them. You use them because you need to shoot to a level of precision that you can't if you don't use them.

For most people under most plausible defensive circumstances, more than adequate precision is obtainable through good stance, a solid focus on the target, and a grasp that keeps the gun from moving when the trigger is pressed. It's only when the target dictates a greater level of precision (such as when the distance to the target requires more precise alignment) that the sights are truly needed.

Your body's natural threat reactions are likely to make it quite difficult for you to use your sights during a lethal fight. It's not impossible for you to focus on that very small piece of metal you're holding at the end of your arm, but from a scientific standpoint it's unlikely. If you train yourself to always use the sights because you can, when your body's natural threat reactions have been initiated and it is difficult or impossible for your eyes to focus on the sight, your hits will be more a matter of luck than of skill or practice. This is in large part because you didn't practice under the conditions that you'd actually use your skills!

This is why I teach to use your sights when you need to. When the target, because of size or distance, dictates that you need to shoot to a greater level of precision is the time to use your snubby's sights.

How do you go about using them? It comes down to two concepts: sight alignment and sight picture, and how they're used together to help you get your snubby aligned on target.

Sight alignment

Most revolver sights are of the "notch and post" variety. A few snubbies have adjustable sights, but the majority of models have a front blade of some sort (the "post") and a slot machined into the rear of the frame. When you look at them from your shooting position, the front blade appears as a squared-off post, and the rear slot (usually) has a square notch.

Sight alignment means the post is placed in the notch, with the tops even and an equal amount of light on either side of the post. On most snubnose revolvers, when the sights are aligned, the bullet should hit on the top center of the post.

Sight picture

Sight picture, on the other hand, refers to how the combination of post and notch is superimposed on the target. The aligned sights are placed or superimposed on the target so that the bullet will land in the desired place.

Combining proper sight alignment with the correct sight picture should — if you roll the trigger straight back without disturbing that alignment — result in the bullet landing exactly where you expected.

Errors in sight alignment

If the tops of the sights aren't even, or if there is more light on one side of the post than the other, your shots will land somewhere other than where you planned. If the front sight is placed too high or too low in the notch, the bullets will impact higher or lower than intended (respectively).

If the post isn't centered in the notch -- if there is an unequal amount of light on the sides -- your shots will land to the side with less "space."

This all sounds more complex than it really is! As you'll learn, there is a certain amount of tolerance in sight alignment that will land your shots within the area of precision dictated by the target. How much tolerance you have depends on the size of the target and the distance to the target. Small targets at longer distances have less tolerance for error and require you to apply more control over your snubby to get accurate hits.

Target focus

The mantra for sight use has always been to "focus on the front sight." Here's where I break from the orthodoxy!

It's useful to remember that if you need to use your sights, it will be because you need to stop an attacker. You'll likely be under your body's natural threat reactions and find it difficult to focus (physically and psychologically) on anything other than the threat you're facing. What are the chances you'll be able to shift your focus from your attacker to a tiny piece of metal at the end of your arm? Not high.

But in most cases you don't need to focus on the front sight to use your sights properly! If you're focused on your attacker (or the target), you can align your sights correctly and superimpose (place) them on your target. They'll just be a little blurry, that's all. You can keep your focus on your target and still discern when your sights are in alignment and easily place them correctly on the point you need to hit.

In fact, some people actually shoot better this way than with a traditional front sight focus, because using the sights in any manner comes down to balancing tradeoffs.

Trading errors

If you focus on your front sight, your target will be blurry. If you focus on your target, your sights will be blurry. No matter what you do, something is going to be blurry. That's just how optical systems work.

If your target is blurred, it will be harder to place your sights precisely on your target. And if you can't clearly see the point you need to hit, it's harder to put a bullet there. You'll have what's known as a "superimposition error."

On the other hand, if you focus on your target, your sights will be blurry. It will be harder to align your sights precisely, leading to what's known as a "superposition error."

With normal handgun sights, you always have one error or the other. In practice, I've found the two errors are roughly equal at any plausible (and even some implausible) shooting distance. In other words, you can trade a superimposition error for a superposition error and end up with substantially equal results.

Simply put, focusing on the target and letting your sights be a little blurry has pretty much the same effect on your precision as doing the opposite. The big difference is focusing on the target will likely be easier when you're under the influence of a natural threat reaction. Focusing on the target and superimposing your blurred-but-aligned sights on top of it is more congruent with how science says the body operates than using the traditional "focus on the front sight" target-shooting technique.

The solution for aging eyes and glasses

If, like me, your eyesight is changing — and particularly if you use bifocals or progressive lenses — it may be physically impossible for you to use your sights at all (at least in anything resembling a solid shooting stance.) You may have been frustrated at your declining skill level, and perhaps have even invested in new sights that you can "see more easily." Again, if you're like me and most of my students, nothing has really helped.

You may find that adopting a target focus while using your sights solves your problems and makes you able to shoot precisely again. In fact, one reason I started looking into the notion of target-focused shooting with sights was because of my own eyesight! The orthodoxy told me I needed to "focus harder" on my front sight or get bigger front sights (which invariably increase the magnitude of alignment and placement errors). None of it worked until I realized something needed to be in focus to make the sights work, and if it couldn't be my front sight the only other choice was the target.

I've had many students suddenly able to shoot to greater degrees of precision than they previously could, simply by changing their focus.

Training out of bad habits

The hardest part of keeping a target focus is undoing previous training. With unsighted fire, covered in the previous section, it's not a problem for most people because not using the sights at all is easier than using them differently. But using the sights is something anyone who's ever been to a class has learned to do. (If you've never had formal instruction, this is going to be a lot easier for you!)

You need to train yourself out of the habit of shifting your focus to the gun and work to keep it where your body will want it to be: on the threat. Students making the transition from the old-fashioned method to the target-focused method often can't bring themselves to focus on the target, and try not to focus on the sight, so they end up compromising by focusing somewhere in the middle. This leads to nothing being in focus, and poor results.

Give it time. Think about looking through your sights, not at them. Focus on your threat, the spot where you want to hit, and keep your focus there as you align and superimpose your blurry sights on that spot and fire the shot.

The narrow blade problem

A common circumstance under which a target focus will fail miserably is when using one of the older Smith & Wesson snubbies with the thin front blade. In the 1960s and 1970s (perhaps a bit later), S&W made several of their snubnose models with an extra-narrow front blade. A normal front blade is usually about 1/8 inch (.125 inch) wide, but these were approximately half that width! They disappear to nothing unless you're looking directly at them, and even then they have a habit of disappearing against a similarly lit target. They're awful under all conditions, but worse when focused on the target.

In the section on Modifications I go into some detail about these narrow-blade models and what can be done to fix them, but frankly, if you have one of those snubbies, it's best to replace it with a gun that has better sights to start.

Are your sights regulated?

When the bullet hits where the sights are pointed, the sights are said to be "regulated." You'd be surprised how many snubbies come from the factory with unregulated or poorly regulated sights!

It's easy to test for sight regulation. Make a small dot in the center of a plain piece of paper or the backside of a target. Stand about 15 feet from the target and, using the dot as your aiming point, fire at least three rounds as precisely as you can. You want a nice group so you can separate shooting problems from sight adjustment problems. Don't look where the bullets are hitting; aim each shot at the dot.

When you're finished, you should have a nice cluster of shots somewhere on the target. If your shots aren't clustered in a group, you need more work on your shooting skills!

If your cluster is on or very close to your aiming dot, your sights are well regulated. The farther the group is from the aiming dot, the more adjustment needs to be made to the sights.

If the group is a bit high or low, but pretty close with regard to the left-right plane (called "windage"), you may be able to change ammunition to a heavier or lighter bullet. Because the weight and velocity of the bullet changes its trajectory, some loads shoot to different points of aim than others. Many older .38 Special snubbies were regulated at the factory for standard-velocity 158-grain bullets, while many newer models have been regulated for 135-grain bullets. Changing the load often corrects these elevation discrepancies.

If the group is noticeably off in windage, and you don't have one of the uncommon models with adjustable sights, you'll probably need to take the gun to a gunsmith to have the error corrected.

The "Six-O'clock Hold"

I always hesitate to talk about this old concept, but it's still out there courtesy of some very out-of-date books (and in some cases, very out-of-date instructors). You may run into it and be confused, so in the interest of your complete education, I'm including it here!

An old sighting method popular around the middle of the last century, the "Six-O'clock Hold," came from the practice of bullseye shooting: a formal, highly choreographed sport in which targets are shot at long distances and scored. The center of the official bullseye target was (and still is) a bold solid circle bullseye surrounded by scoring rings. At the regulation shooting distance and when the shooter's eyes were focused on the front sight, the only thing that stood out on the fuzzy target was that solid black area.

Bullseye competitors soon learned that their black sights simply disappeared against the black center of the target, which is where they actually wanted to hit. This combination of black on fuzzy black made it difficult to both align their sights and place them on the target. Their solution was to adjust their sights so they could aim at the bottom edge of the bullseye, where their sights stood out against the off-white target, while the bullets would hit well above their aim point and into the center of the bullseye. In other words, they were aiming a known distance from where they wanted to hit and adjusted their sights to compensate.

In practice they would align their sights and superimpose them on the target so the bold black bullseye sat perched in the top center of their front sight post. This gave them the best of all possible worlds: a very sharp front sight, which reduced errors in alignment, and a better-defined target to reduce the errors in sight picture. That's how bullseye matches were won!

In defensive shooting this proved to be a poor practice. Bad guys don't have target markings, and trying to remember how far below the target to aim so the bullets would hit in the correct place really isn't possible under the stress and confusion of an attack.

For self-defense use, a snubby's sights should be adjusted so the bullet hits where the top edge of the front sight post is placed. This is often referred to as "point of aim/point of impact" sighting. Snubbies with fixed sights that don't hit to point of aim should be taken to a gunsmith for adjustment or replacement.

* — *Source: "Worlds Collide: Countering Sight Fixation" video from Springfield Armory, https://www.youtube.com/watch?v=ij7u-e0Z4EU&t=26s*

Proper sight alignment and sight picture: bullet will land in the center of the bullseye

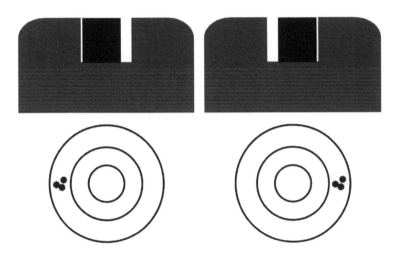

Errors in windage: if the blade isn't centered in the notch, the bullets will hit left or right of intended point of aim

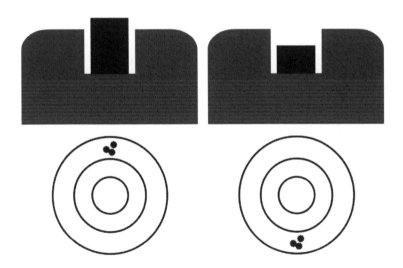

Errors in elevation: the front blade being higher or lower than the top of the rear notch will cause the shots to impact high or low

RELOADING THE SNUBBY

In my previous revolver books I spent some time on the subject of reloading the revolver. In the years since those books were written I've come to view the act of reloading in a very different light, and as a result my recommendations have changed. Because of the goal being efficiency in training, and in recognition of the plausibility of needing the skill, I've de-emphasized the idea of extensively practicing the snubby reload.

The real need for reloading

The reality is that reloading a handgun — any handgun — is a skill rarely used in defensive shooting.

It's difficult to find examples in the world of private-sector self defense where a defender initiated a reload during a fight. In those few cases where someone did reload their gun, it's almost impossible to find a case where that reload affected the outcome of the incident. If you go back to the section about Plausibility and consider the frequency of the need for reloading, it becomes clear that a reload during a defensive shooting isn't at all likely. It has happened so rarely, in fact, that it's only barely plausible. Given that, it seems a waste of time to practice something you'll probably never use.

Remember, though, that one of the criteria for determining plausibility is a combination of factors that could believably occur. When you consider the low capacity of the snubnose revolver and combine that with the increase in multiple-assailant crimes across the country, that combination raises the plausibility of needing to reload during an incident. Looked at in that light, the need for the skill of reloading the snubby is certainly plausible. The issue is that it's not worth devoting a lot of time or effort to.

Luckily, almost any amount of training or practice will result in your experiencing an empty gun and needing to reload. If you go to the range with a box of ammo and a five-shot snubby, you're going to need to reload ten times! Those ten times are opportunities to get in "free" practice, meaning you'll be able to work on a skill without taking time or energy away from practicing another (more vital) skill. Since reloading has to be done during any practice, doing it properly every time gives you an opportunity to engage in contextual practice of the skill.

The snubby isn't easy to reload

The snubnose revolver is more dependent on fine motor control for reloading than the semiautomatic pistol is. At the same time, you're likely to experience loss of fine motor control when your body is reacting to a threat. It's therefore probably a good idea to reduce reliance on fine muscle movements to the greatest degree possible — that is, if you want to reload your snubby reliably!

As it happens, there is more than one way to reload the revolver. An autoloading pistol is easy: you push a button and shove in a new magazine. There isn't a lot of variation in the process. With the snubby, however, there is. Because of the amount of interaction with the gun, the snubnose revolver can be reloaded in many different ways — and there are sometimes great debates on which method is "best"!

Complicating matters is that some methods dramatically increase the risk of malfunctions, such as having a case caught under the extractor (which isn't quickly or easily fixed during a fight). Unlike the autopistol, a successful snubby reload is far more dependent on your skill for success.

I've experimented with reloading methods extensively over the years and come up with some specifics on how best to reload the snubby, avoiding fine motor skills wherever possible and adopting procedures that reduce the risk of fouling the reload through bad technique.

A note for experienced snubnose shooters

If you've been shooting snubbies for a while, you may already know a reload method. I'm not a fan of re-training previous learned skills unless a compelling reason to do so exists and the benefit of the re-training exceeds the time and effort spent. In the case of the snubnose reload procedure, I'm happy with any reload method that incorporates all of the following:

1. The ejector rod is slapped, not merely pushed.
2. The cylinder is immobilized (kept from turning or closing back into the frame).
3. Putting ammunition into the chambers is done with your strong (shooting) hand, for the best control over the most delicate part of the operation.

If your reloading method already does those things, you probably don't need to read any further!

Reloading the snubby

As I mentioned, my preferred reloading method reduces fine motor control as much as possible while avoiding the common user-induced errors that can delay or even prevent a reload from succeeding.

Since reloading a revolver is dexterity intensive, this method uses your shooting (strong) hand to do the most delicate task: inserting rounds into the chambers. Many people espouse that it's faster to do this with the weak hand, but in the stress of a fight it makes little sense to assign the most important and difficult task to the hand least suited to doing it. This method may not be the absolute fastest, but it is the surest (and is still very quick!)

Recognizing that you need to reload your snubby is different than what you experience with a semiautomatic pistol: The cue that a reload is necessary is the hammer falling and no shot being fired (the "click" sound). While it's possible to run into a dud cartridge in the first couple of chambers, your increasing experience will tell you whether it's a misfire (and you should pull the trigger again) or an empty gun (you need to reload). If the misfire happens near the last round, always reload as a matter of practicality.

Here's how it's done:

1) As soon as you recognize that you need to reload, your trigger finger moves to the rest position (on the revolver's frame, above the trigger). Your focus should remain on the threat as much as possible while the reload is accomplished. In other words, you should be able to complete the reload without looking at the gun. This is harder with the snubnose revolver than with the autoloading pistol, but it's doable with practice.

2) Bring the snubby back toward the ready position, which gives you better strength and greater control. As the gun comes back, your support hand moves forward so you can hold the cylinder between your thumb on one side and your fore and middle fingers on the opposite side. Point your shooting-hand thumb forward where it can easily operate the cylinder release.

3) Hold the cylinder between your thumb and fingers and start to rotate the frame of the revolver away from it, which opens the cylinder and allows the muzzle to point up. (If using a Colt, reach under the cylinder release and push the thumb latch as the revolver's muzzle rotates up.) The key here is to eject the spent cases only after the muzzle is pointed at the sky.

4) You're now holding the snubby with your support hand, and the cylinder has been immobilized between your fingers so it can't turn or close. Flatten your shooting hand and swiftly strike the ejector rod one time with your palm. This accelerates the brass and tends to throw it clear of the cylinder, even with short ejector rods. Velocity is more important than force, and you should strike the ejector rod one time only. If any cases fail to clear the cylinder, multiple ejections are not likely to clear them but will significantly raise the risk of a case-under-extractor jam.

5) Rotate the muzzle so it's pointing toward the ground as much as possible. You'll probably find you need to drop the gun down to your mid-abdominal level to do this comfortably. Tuck your elbows in a bit to help immobilize the gun relative to your body. As you're doing this, your shooting hand retrieves the spare ammunition. Whether you carry your spare ammunition in a speed-loader, Speed Strip, or just loose, insert the new rounds into the chambers.

6) Once the rounds are in the cylinder (and you've dropped any reloading aid), re-establish a firing grasp with your shooting hand and roll your hands together as if closing a book. This closes the cylinder and lets you get your support hand back into a shooting grasp. The revolver is now reloaded and ready to be shot again (if necessary).

Tips on speedloader use

The most efficient way to recharge a snubnose revolver is no doubt the speedloader. The speedloader's big advantage is that it inserts all the rounds into the cylinder at the same time. A speedloader is to a revolver what a spare magazine is to a pistol, but the speedloader requires a little more attention to technique than the pistol's magazine.

1) The best and easiest way to hold the speedloader is to grasp it by the body. Do not grasp the speedloader by the knob, because it slows handling and raises the risk that you'll release the rounds accidentally, such as while still in your pocket.

2) Sometimes the bullet noses line up perfectly with the chambers and drop in easily, but sometimes that doesn't happen. Develop the habit of rapidly rotating the speedloader slightly in one direction then the other. It's more of a wiggle than a turn. When you feel the bullets dropping into the chambers, manipulate the speedloader to release the rounds.

3) After the rounds have been released, pull the speedloader straight back from the cylinder to allow the rims of the cartridges to clear the loader's housing. This prevents jams due to speedloader tilt (a very common issue).

Practicing the reload

As noted, if you spend any time on the range practicing your defensive shooting skills, you'll eventually experience an empty snubby. Remember that it's your recognition of the condition of an empty gun that gives you the stimulus to respond using your practiced reloading skill. You'll have ample opportunities to practice reloading your snubnose during the normal course of shooting, and it's not necessary to set up special "reloading drills."

Your reloading repetitions are only of real value if your reloads are not choreographed. By that, I mean your reloads happen at your recognition of an empty gun rather than at a predetermined point. The best way to do this is to shoot exercises that don't have specific round counts or exercises where the number of rounds being shot isn't known until the shooting actually starts. Being surprised by the need to reload is different than planning a reload at some arbitrary point and is more congruent with the conditions under which you're likely to need to reload your snubby.

Again: it's not necessary to perform special "reloading drills." If you shoot often enough, you'll find yourself with an empty gun frequently, giving you all the time you need to practice reloading!

Additional thoughts on speedloaders There are two broad categories of speedloaders: those that require a turning motion of some sort to release the rounds (such as the speedloaders from HKS and 5 Star), and those that require a pushing motion (Safariland, JetLoader, and S.L. Variant).

I find the push-type easier and faster to use, because the motion to release the rounds is the same as the motion that inserted the speedloader into the cylinder. Releasing the rounds is simply a continuation of that motion, making them very intuitive.

The turn-type speedloaders require you to grasp the operating knob and turn in the correct direction. I've owned some HKS speedloaders for over 20 years and still turn the knob the wrong way to release the rounds! The push-type models are unambiguous and easier to master.

Although I own many different models of push-type speedloaders, I've found the Safariland loaders to be the most rugged and the most widely available. The only time I use a twist speedloader is if Safariland doesn't make a model that fits the specific snubby I'm using.

Reload starts by grasping cylinder between thumb and fingers of support hand while operating cylinder release. Cylinder remains in grasp as it's opened; fingers of support hand push thorugh the frame window.

Once cylinder is opened muzzle is turned upward as shooting hand flattens to rapidly strike ejector rod. Note that cylinder is firmly immobolized between the thumb and fingers of support hand.

After empties have been ejected muzzle is pointed at the ground and spare ammunition inserted. Cylinder is still immobilized, a necessity if using turn-type speedloaders.

Once ammunition is in cylinder and the loading tool dropped, the shooting hand re-establishes a shooting grasp and the cylinder is closed.

DRAWING & REHOLSTERING

One of the huge benefits of the snubnose revolver is it's efficient to get into action. It has no external safeties or decockers or other nonsense to worry about: just get a good shooting grasp and pull the trigger! At least, that's how it seems.

Getting the concealed snubby out of its holster and into a position where it can be effectively fired is the key to taking advantage of the revolver's efficiency. Drawing the snubnose is a primary defensive shooting skill, and one you should spend time and effort to master.

"Drawstroke" is the term we use to encompass the physical acts of getting to the gun, getting it out of the holster safely, and putting it into a position where it can be fired. It needs to be done as safely yet as quickly as possible, and should be consistent with the other gun-handling skills you're practicing.

As you read the following, keep in mind that you'll be drawing the gun and moving through the ready position into full extension.

Components of the drawstroke

I don't normally take an overly mathematical approach to defensive shooting, but there are five components to the snubby draw, three of which you've already been introduced to in the section on Extension. They are, in order:

GRASP — Get your shooting hand onto the grip of the snubby. Your hand should be in a firing grasp before you proceed further. You should have a solid grasp on the gun, with your fingers properly wrapped around the grip and your shooting hand thumb curling down, before you pull the gun from the holster. If your holster has any retention devices, such as a hammer strap, they need to be defeated as you get your grasp on the gun.

UP — Pull the snubby out of the holster and bring it as far away from the holster (usually up) as you comfortably can, but don't blow out your elbow or shoulder trying to exaggerate the position. Keep the barrel parallel to your thighs at all times. This prevents the muzzle from being pointed at any part of your body, and is key to drawing the gun safely from disadvantaged positions (which we won't be covering in this book, but it's best to build safe habits from the beginning!)

ORIENT — Point the muzzle at the target (or threat), being careful not to let its path cross any part of your body. You'll end up with the snubby in a position very similar to the ready position: the gun will be roughly around the middle of the torso, your elbows close to your body, and the barrel roughly parallel to the ground. As I said above, you're moving through the ready position during the draw.

EXTEND — As you've already learned, the gun is extended from the ready position toward your target. You should end up with your arms extended an equal amount and as far as possible. The elbows should ideally be in their locked position before you touch the trigger.

TOUCH or TOUCH & FIRE — Place your finger on the trigger and smoothly increase the pressure applied by your trigger finger until the shot fires.

Practicing the drawstroke

When you first practice drawing your snubby, do each component as a discrete, single step so you become familiar with how the gun should safely move. (Even if you're an experienced shooter, if you switch holster positions or carry methods, start over again, practicing the steps so they come naturally.) With each repetition, slightly increase your speed by reducing the amount of time between each step.

After you've become familiar with the individual steps, perform the entire draw sequence as one continuous movement. Start slowly and build your speed only as you become more competent at performing the draw safely. It's tempting to push yourself to go faster right off the bat, but focusing too much on the speed of the draw in these beginning stages often leads to unsafe habits.

Remember: the key is to draw the gun through the ready position and extend on the target. If you understand the draw sequence as the logical development of the extension, the gun will come smoothly out of the holster, through the ready position and into extension on target.

Focus on the threat!

Don't lose sight of the reason for drawing your snubby in the first place! You're practicing your draw so you can efficiently respond to an attack you didn't see coming ahead of time. Your body will want to focus all its attention on the threat, and you want it to do so! Practice the draw sequence as you're likely to use it: with your eyes and attention focused on the target.

Drawing from concealment

During your initial practice sessions it's best to draw the snubby from an unconcealed condition, without any concealment or "cover" garments. After you've become competent with the draw, then add in whatever concealment clothing you'll be wearing when you carry your snubby in public. We'll cover the specifics of how to do that in a later chapter.

How do you handle the added complication of cover clothing? Think about getting to the gun in the same way you get to your wallet or car keys. When you reach into your hip pocket for your wallet, do you obsess about how to get past your jacket or shirt? At the risk of using a clichéd phrase, you just do it! Similarly, think about getting your hand onto your snubby as efficiently as you can, without grabbing any clothing along the way. Lots of people have written lots of gun magazine articles about special techniques to move cover garments out of the way for a "faster draw," but I've found that focusing on getting the hand to the gun strips away a lot of the nonsense.

Because of the many different ways a snubnose can be carried, and the un-told variations in cover garments, it's difficult to go into great detail about any specific method. If you're carrying in a pocket holster, how you get your hand to your gun is different than if you're carrying in an inside-the-waistband appendix holster, but if you think about "hand to gun," most of the issues fall by the wayside.

Re-holstering

Inserting a handgun into a holster, whether re-holstering after shooting or just putting the gun on first thing in the morning, is the most dangerous part of routine handling. This is when most unintentional discharges happen, and consequently when most self-inflicted wounds occur.

The first and most important thing to understand is, there is no trophy for getting your snubby into its holster the fastest. Unlike drawing, which you should practice to do as swiftly as possible, the act of re-holstering needs to be more deliberate. There is no need to "speed holster"! Holstering should be done reluctantly, as if your fight might flare up again (which has been known to happen from time to time).

Think about it this way: you've just been forced to draw (and likely shoot) your snubnose because someone tried to maim or kill you. Your body's natural threat reactions have been activated, you're breathing hard, and feel more shaken than you've ever been. Why would you want to get your rescue tool back into its storage place quickly? Naturally, you don't — which is why my advice is to practice holstering both reluctantly and deliberately.

How to holster safely

You've practiced bringing the snubby back into the ready position after shooting. If you intend to re-holster, pause slightly. This gives you a chance to collect your thoughts, and if in an actual shooting incident, it gives you the opportunity to look around for other threats you might need to deal with (or police officers shouting orders at you). Make sure your trigger finger is outside the trigger guard, on the frame below the cylinder.

After you've consciously decided to re-holster (holstering should never be an unconscious act), keep the barrel parallel to your thighs and point the muzzle at the ground. Be sure you're not pointing the muzzle at your own feet!

If you can do so safely, look at your holster and ensure no clothing or other items are obstructing the holster's opening. Obstructions are second only to a poorly controlled trigger finger in causing accidental discharges! Insert the gun slowly into the holster (and secure any retention devices you might have). Once the gun is holstered, tuck in any loose clothing.

Focus on keeping the barrel parallel to your body. A common issue I see with students wearing holsters behind the hip is canting the muzzle toward the side of the abdomen while holstering. That creates an extremely dangerous condition, and the only prevention is to pay strict attention to the orientation of the gun during the holstering process. Again: reluctantly and deliberately!

GRASP: Get a solid firing grasp on the gun; defeat any holster retention devices

UP: Bring the gun out of the holster as far as is comfortable, keeping the muzzle parallel to the thighs

ORIENT: point the muzzle at the target, taking the shortest path to doing so

EXTEND (TOUCH and FIRE): extend through the ready position and into a stable shooting stance

SOME THOUGHTS ABOUT TARGETS

The defensive training target needs to do several things. First, it must dictate the level of precision to which you need to shoot, and it should do so unambiguously and unconditionally. What do I mean by that?

By unambiguously, I mean the precision to which you need to shoot should be indicated in an obvious way. The target shouldn't be testing your eyesight or color perception, because at this stage those things aren't important. What is important is that the target helps you develop your ability to recognize the degree of precision to which you need to shoot, and to link that with a specific application of skill necessary to deliver that level of precision. Later in your skill development, you can use those links to help determine how much skill you need to reliably hit a target that might not be so clear.

(Those of you who have seen the original Star Wars movie might remember the scene where the rebel pilots are briefing about how to destroy the Death Star, and that they needed to deliver their bombs into an opening two meters wide. One pilot says it's impossible, but Luke Skywalker compares the opening to "womp rats" he used to shoot back home. That's the concept: relate an unknown to a similar known, but you can only do that if you've developed the recognition and recall first. An unambiguous target helps you do that.)

By unconditionally, I mean the target gives you a digital result: either you hit the target at which you are aiming or you didn't. The target should have no variable scoring, such as a "10" ring surrounded by an "8" ring surrounded by a "5" ring. If it does, the tendency (and it's incredibly strong) is to rationalize a miss by thinking, "I still got 80% of the score" or "It still would have hurt the bad guy." Both those rationalizations sabotage your skill development because they prevent a solid link between your application of skill and a definite result.

In order to develop good defensive skills and test their application, the ideal target will have a roughly chest-sized main target area and several smaller precision target areas that are at least one-third the size of the main target. The first exists because that's the likely amount of precision an attacker will demand from you. The others exist because you may be required to shoot at a smaller or more distant target, which will require a greater level of precision. (Review the section on Accuracy and Precision if this is unclear.)

A good training target should be arranged in such a way that you can randomize what you'll shoot next. This will become clearer as you read through the various exercises, but a key function of skill development is to allow your brain to make decisions as problems are presented. Shooting the same thing all the time, or the same things in the same order, doesn't develop that ability nearly as well as randomized and interleaved experiences. A good target has enough variation that you can change what you're shooting in such a way that you can't easily anticipate what comes next.

Finally, from strictly an efficiency standpoint, the ideal target has several of each of those target areas so you can shoot quite a bit without constantly changing targets. (If you're an instructor, this translates to less class time spent in administrative tasks and more time shooting!)

My favorite target meets all those criteria and is produced by Law Enforcement Targets (*www.letargets.com*). The Combat Focus Training Target (SKU: CFS-BSP)* has three large target areas and seven much smaller precision target areas. Some are identified by letters, some by numbers, and colors and shapes are mixed in as well. I've been using it for years, and if I were limited to a single target for all my training and teaching activities, I could easily live with it.

Making your own targets

Don't think you have to buy those "special" targets just to make use of the information and exercises in this book! You can certainly make perfectly serviceable targets at home using colored markers and printer paper.

You need to make the following:

1) A large primary target area. One sheet with a largish square of about 8x8 inches is sufficient.

2) Several smaller precision target circles. Draw several circles of roughly 2 inches in diameter. Use different colors if possible, and number each with a number between one and six. Put two non-identical targets on one side of a sheet of paper.

3) Several smaller precision areas with square and triangle shapes, roughly 3 inches on a side. You can use colors or letters (or both) to differentiate these. Put two non-identical targets on one side of a sheet of paper.

That's really all you need. When you get to the range, staple or tape them to a sheet of cardboard: the primary target area near the top and centered, and several of the precision target sheets either alongside or below (depending on the width and length of the facility's target system). You're ready to start training!

Free downloadable targets

If you'd rather not mess with making your own, I've prepared a Target Pak you can print out at home and take to the range. The targets in the Pak combine shapes, colors, numbers, and letters that will allow you to properly randomize your training experience.

Here's the link to download your copies:
www.grantcunningham.com/free-snubnose-targets/

* — *Full disclosure: I had a small hand in helping to develop this target, but I derive no revenue or benefit from your purchasing and using it.*

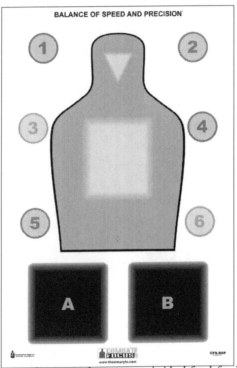

CFS-BSP target from www.letargets.com is ideal for defensive training

RANGE SAFETY AND ETIQUETTE

I realize talking about etiquette seems old-fashioned in this day and age, but range etiquette is important for your training progress, safety, and enjoyment. Over the years I've noticed that the jerks on the range are always the least safe, and paying attention to my own behavior focuses my attention on my own safety habits.

Safety rules

Most ranges have a sheet of safety rules hanging on a wall somewhere. Sometimes there are four rules, sometimes a few more, and sometimes a list as long as your arm (and for once, that's not a figure of speech!). If you pay attention to the three rules I talked about in the Safe Handling section, you'll be well ahead of almost everyone you encounter.

Because they're so important, let's go over them again:

1. Always keep the muzzle pointed in a generally safe direction.
What is a generally safe direction? One in which, should the gun fire, you will not hurt someone else. On a shooting range, the berm or bullet trap behind the target is a generally safe direction, and depending on the surface the ground may be as well. There may be other generally safe directions which are location specific. Of course other shooters, staff or onlookers are never a generally safe direction!

2. Always keep your trigger finger outside of the trigger guard unless you're actually shooting.
The preferred place is on the frame above the trigger. In the case of the snubnose revolver, that means the frame space below the cylinder and above the trigger. It does not mean resting on the trigger guard itself!

3. Always remember you are in possession of a device that, if used recklessly or negligently, can injure or kill you or someone else.

This is the "big picture" of safety. It encompasses all those other safety rules you might see on posters and signs at the range: making sure of your target; making sure you know where the bullets will land; using the right ammunition for the gun; keeping your gun out of the hands of unauthorized users; etc. It is intended to instill in your mind an attitude about safety without providing an endless checklist of items to remember.

The individual range may have specific procedures posted that you need to follow. While not universal safety rules like those above, they contribute to your safe and enjoyable use of the facilities. Familiarize yourself with how your range operates and what other users expect of you.

Safety as a concept

Safety is more than just a bunch of rules that you regurgitate: it's a way of looking at risk and managing your exposure to it. From that standpoint, the value of anything you do has to greatly outweigh the risks you assume in doing it.

A good illustration of this idea is wearing ear protection at the range. We know that exposure to loud noises like gunshots quickly damages hearing. We also know this damage is cumulative and irreversible. If you were to go out and simply start shooting (especially on an indoor range), it would not take long to lose a significant amount of your hearing. The risks of hearing damage far outweigh the benefit you'd get by practicing.

That's why, whenever you go to the range, wearing ear protection is a non-negotiable rule. It attenuates the sound pulses that reach your ears to such a degree that you can shoot all day long, every day, without any perceptible damage to your hearing. The value of your practice, or even the recreational value from "plinking," now greatly exceeds the risk you took — all because of the earmuffs or plugs!

The same is true of wearing eye protection when you shoot. Always wear personal protective equipment (PPE) for your ears and eyes!

Getting along with fellow range patrons

Most ranges have specific procedures for range operation. For instance, if your targets are hung on fixed (non-retractable) frames, everyone needs to stop shooting at the same time (called a "cease fire"), unload their guns, and not handle any firearms while others go downrange to change the targets. You may not need to change yours, but if that's the case don't be handling your snubby behind the shooting line! Stand well back from the counter where the empty guns are lying.

Be sure to keep an eye on others who may also be hanging back (or those who return before the others have finished with their targets). While thankfully an uncommon occurrence, guns have been stolen at such times.

Also watch what's happening behind the line. Many years ago, I was at a private shooting club when a cease-fire was called to change targets. Six of us were using the range that day, and five changed our targets. Three had gone back to the shooting line, leaving me and one other person at the target frames, when I suddenly heard the crack of a rifle discharging behind me! I dropped to the ground and looked at the firing line I'd left behind, and sure enough the guy who hadn't changed his target had decided to start shooting. Those who'd already returned ran over and stopped him. They also told him to leave and not come back, which he wisely did before I could run the 100 yards back to get my hands around his neck!

If you arrive at such a range, wait patiently for others to reach a stopping point so you can hang your first target. Don't be a jerk about it. Get your guns and ammunition out, speedloaders prepared, and generally organize yourself. (Of course, do all of this without pointing guns at the other shooters on the line!) The other patrons will usually ask if you want a cease-fire, and the polite response is, "Whenever it's convenient for you." If you're one of the people shooting when someone shows up, it's your place to ask the newcomer if they'd like a cease-fire.

Particularly if you're shooting on an indoor range, pay attention to what the other patrons are doing. Not everyone is at the range to practice their defensive shooting skills. Some people might be calmly and slowly shooting to produce the best groups they can, and others may be plinking. You'll be shooting rapid, multiple shots that might disturb their concentration or fun. If that's the case, pick a shooting lane as far away from them as you can. It's the polite thing to do, and greatly reduces the imposition of "no rapid fire" rules.

Shooting in wilderness areas

In the section on Special Considerations for Restricted Ranges, I suggest that heading to a wilderness shooting area might be a workable option for some people. I also caution you to never go alone.

While in most cases you won't see anyone else at such places, in many instances people have been robbed of their guns. Firearms are prime theft targets, because they have both utility and intrinsic value to criminals. An isolated location where people are known to have these high-value items in their possession can be a tempting target for an enterprising thief, and robberies (some with fatalities) have happened. This isn't intended to make you paranoid, but just be aware you might be a target and that there is strength in having others with you.

When I've been shooting at such locations I've made sure that at least one of us always has a loaded firearm. We take turns shooting, and part of the observer/training partner's job is to pay attention to who else might be showing up.

Non-confrontational robberies have occurred, too. Leaving guns on the ground as you go downrange to change targets is a bad idea. I've known people who came back to their shooting position only to find their gun(s) mysteriously missing! Keep your guns with you (and your car locked) in any such remote location.

These are relatively rare incidents, but they have happened and should be guarded against. If you're shooting at an isolated location always take someone with you, always have a loaded firearm on your person, and never leave any guns unattended. It's no different than living in some urban areas, but it's easy to get complacent when you're out in nature. Don't let your guard down just because the trees are pretty and the birds are singing!

GRASP PRESSURE EXERCISE

As noted in the section on Trigger Control, a solid grasp is vital to being able to manipulate the trigger of the snubnose revolver without moving the muzzle off target. You'll be applying much more force to the trigger than the gun weighs — in the worst-case but very common scenario, as much as 12 times the gun's weight! Without your strong grasp, the muzzle can (and probably will) be thrown off its alignment with the target, and inaccurate shots will result.

Controlling recoil

At the same time, if you're forced to use your snubby to defend your life, you're likely to shoot multiple rounds very quickly. That's the nature of defensive encounters: it usually takes more than one round to reliably incapacitate an attacker, and you don't know ahead of time how many you'll need to fire. You also want to get those rounds on to the target as quickly as you can, because the sooner he collapses, the better!

One of the snubby's negative attributes is that it has a sharper recoil impulse than a full-size revolver. Ultra-lightweight snubbies generate recoil that can be difficult even for an experienced shooter to handle! Higher levels of recoil during rapid shooting make keeping shots on target a very difficult task.

A solid grasp not only helps you with good trigger control, it also helps you manage even the fierce recoil of the lightest snubbies. A solid grasp makes it possible to make those rapid, multiple, accurate hits more reliably under a wider range of conditions.

But most of the people I see in my classes grasp their snubbies far less firmly than they actually can. This gives them an unrealistic notion of what they can actually do and how they can actually shoot. Teaching them how to reliably achieve an optimal grasp solves many shooting problems, and gives them a better understanding of their own shooting ability — which, in turn, means they'll shoot more confidently and make better decisions about how they're going to shoot when the time comes.

The Grasp Pressure exercise will help you learn what your optimal grasp is, make it easier to come to your optimal grasp, improve your balance of speed and precision, and over time will improve your grasp. This is a non-shooting drill and can be done anywhere you have a safe backstop.

Procedure

Get a proper two-handed firing grasp on the gun (see the section on Grasp for the details). Hold the gun in the ready position, finger off the trigger, then start increasing the pressure (squeeze) in both hands. As you increase your grasp pressure, at some point your muscles will start trembling from the effort; you'll see the gun visibly shake. When you see that tremble, relax your hand pressure just enough to stop the tremors. The resulting pressure level is your optimal grasp at that point in time. Hold that optimal pressure for about five seconds, concentrating on what it feels like. Then relax.

Rest for a few seconds, then repeat the exercise. Focus on memorizing the pressure at which you can hold without muscle tremor.

Once you've done that a few times and have a good feeling for what your optimal grasp pressure is, extend out into your shooting position (finger still off the trigger), rapidly increasing your grasp pressure as the gun comes into your line of sight. By the time you reach full extension, your grasp pressure should be at your memorized optimal level, without any trembling. Hold that for a few seconds, then bring the gun back into the ready position and relax. Repeat this until you can automatically come to that optimal grasp pressure without needing to consciously monitor the process.

Even if you've been shooting for some time, you probably don't hold your handgun with anything close to the amount of pressure that you really can. Most people are surprised at how tightly they can actually grasp their gun, and their shooting invariably improves as a result.

This exercise can be very tiring, so don't overdo it. Over time, you'll likely find that this exercise increases your hand and forearm strength. The key is frequent but short sessions.

EXTEND-TOUCH-FIRE EXERCISE

This is a deceptively simple yet important exercise!

Extend-Touch-Fire is the most fundamental exercise in this book, because the act of getting the gun into a shooting position is the same whether the gun is being carried, retrieved from storage, or when having already shot but finding the need to shoot again. It's also the second half of drawing the gun from the holster (see the section Drawing and Reholstering).

The goal for this exercise is to integrate all the actions that need to be done as you bring the gun into a shooting position:

- the increase to optimal grasp pressure
- bringing the gun into and parallel with your line of sight
- reaching and holding at maximum extension
- the proper timing of getting your finger onto the trigger
- the act of firing a shot as soon as all of the foregoing has occurred

Despite shooting snubbies for many years, I still occasionally do this exercise to make sure I haven't developed any lazy habits! It's helpful to do this with a partner, but not necessary.

Procedure

1) Start by standing with your loaded gun in the ready position, three to four yards from the target. Your trigger finger should off the trigger and resting on the frame under the cylinder. Your target should be approximately 10x10 inches to represent the upper chest area of a human attacker.

2) Get into your natural, neutral shooting stance: square to the target, knees flexed, bowing slightly from the waist.

3) Focus on the center of the target area you need to hit and stay focused on that point.

4) If you don't have a partner, think the command EXTEND and bring the gun into and parallel with your line of sight as you extend your arms out and come to your optimal grasp.

5) On the command TOUCH, put your finger on the trigger, paying careful attention to the ideal finger position (crease of the first joint on or next to the trigger face). Don't apply pressure. Just allow your finger to touch the trigger enough to feel your finger position.

6) On the command FIRE, smoothly and rapidly increase the pressure you're applying to the trigger, directing the trigger straight back toward your nose, until the gun fires. One shot only!

7) After the shot is fired, take your finger off the trigger, rest it on the frame under the cylinder, and come back to the ready position. Be sure to relax your grasp when you reach the ready position.

Repeat until the cylinder is empty. If you feel the need for more repetitions, reload the snubby and repeat.

Start out slowly, but with each repetition, reduce the time between the commands. Each repetition should be a little faster than the previous one, but the steps should still be distinct and separate.

Common issues

The key is to get a smooth extension without the gun "bowling" (dropping down before coming up into your line of sight, like the movements of someone throwing a bowling ball), "flycasting" (the muzzle pointing up as it comes into your line of sight, then dropping down to point at the target), or wobbling when it reaches the limits of your extension (see the section on Extension). The process should be smooth, predictable, and solid.

Remember the escalator analogy: the gun comes up and forward at the same time, and around halfway to full extension, you're walking off the escalator and toward the target.

Evaluation/troubleshooting

Strive for a 100% hit rate. Misses are often caused by not being at full extension when the shot breaks (especially toward the end of the exercise when you're performing the actions in more rapid succession). Many times you won't actually be at full extension when you touch and fire, and you're still moving when the shot breaks.

Another common problem I see in my students is their grasp pressure isn't sufficient to control the gun, or their grasp pressure is still being increased as the trigger is pressed. Make sure your grasp is at your memorized optimum (see the Grasp Pressure exercise) before your arms reach full extension and you touch the trigger.

ONE AT A TIME EXERCISE

This exercise is the logical extension of, and should immediately follow, the Extend-Touch-Fire exercise.

As noted, your first shot is your best opportunity to affect your attacker's ability to hurt you. Making an accurate first shot is important, but it's just as important to make that shot as quickly as you can. The extension to the first shot, whether from ready position or out of the holster, dramatically affects your ability to make an accurate first shot. To develop your ability to make that fast, accurate first shot, you perform the separate movements of the Extend-Touch-Fire exercise as one continuous motion, and the command (if you have a training partner) should be one short, simple word, such as "UP!"

When you hear that command (or if you're alone, have decided to shoot), you extend, touch, and fire in one continuous motion. The actions are no longer distinct and separate; now they're blended together so the act of shooting is a smooth flow of motion. You should not stop moving until just before the shot breaks.

Start slowly, paying attention to making the extension to first shot an unbroken movement. As you gain confidence, increase the speed at which the extension happens — always paying attention to smoothness and being solidly motionless when the shot is fired.

Like the Extend-Touch-Fire exercise, this is shot at three to four yards.

Common issues

This is where I see issues with bowling, flycasting, and wobbling start to crop up. It's important to start slowly as you integrate each of the movements. Trying to go fast before you're ready often results in those common issues. It's helpful to video yourself at this point, looking for small issues with your stance or extension. You may not realize you're flycasting, for instance, but the video on your phone may reveal that's exactly what you're doing!

Evaluation/troubleshooting

These are the same as for the Extend-Touch-Fire exercise.

MULTIPLE SHOTS EXERCISE

This exercise sets the stage for most of the other exercises in this book and is the foundation of realistic defensive shooting.

Most students in most classes, and just about everyone you'll see on shooting ranges, shoot a predictable and repetitive number of rounds every time they extend the gun. The problem is that because they know they're going to shoot, say, two rounds (the well-known "double tap"), they relax after those two rounds. They get used to shooting two rounds and relaxing, over and over again.

When suddenly faced with the surprise of needing to fire a third shot, very often that third round goes out of the target area. They weren't prepared to shoot that round, and their grasp and extension weren't at the same level as the first two shots.

In a defensive shooting, it's impossible to know in advance how many rounds you'll need to fire. Your ability to control your snubby in a rapid string of fire is critical to making every shot count, and setting yourself up for the next shot — whether you need to fire it or not — is the key to being able to deliver as many shots as you need, as rapidly as you can, and make them all accurate.

This drill gives you experience in shooting more than one or two rounds at a time. It's important to maintain your shooting readiness after each shot — posture, grasp pressure, finger position, focus point on the target — so you can make the next shot if you need to. Only after you've decided to stop shooting and the gun is coming back into the ready position do you relax.

Procedure

The Multiple Shots exercise is the same as the One At A Time, except you shoot a random number of rounds between two and five, never repeating the same number of shots twice in a row, as quickly as you can make accurate hits.

After you've shot the number of rounds you decided to fire, bring the gun back into the ready position.

Common issues

At this point, you should have demonstrated the ability to put accurate rounds on target in the previous exercises, so your issues should be related almost exclusively to dealing with recoil.

Things to watch for: It's common to prematurely relax your grasp on the final round. This is common and you'll see it if your last shot is inaccurate. It's also common to start to get out of the natural shooting stance (weight forward, slight crouch) as you prepare to relax. If your last shot lands high, you probably unconsciously started to straighten up as you fired that last round.

Evaluation/troubleshooting

The key to self-troubleshooting is being able to identify whether your missed shots came on the first round or subsequent rounds.

If your first shot is off target, just as in the One At A Time exercise, the cause can be the result of not being at full extension (gun still moving) when the shot is fired; the gun not being in and parallel with your line of sight; or not being at your optimal grasp pressure when you trigger the shot.

Misses on subsequent shots often indicate poor recoil control. Check your stance and extension. Make sure you have a weight-forward bias and your elbows are at full extension and locked into position (if physically possible). Also be sure your shoulders rolled forward; this is an often overlooked detail of the ideal shooting stance. Always check that you're maintaining your optimal grasp pressure throughout the whole string of fire. Adjusting your grasp on your snubby between shots is usually a sign of improper hand positioning or inadequate grasp pressure.

If any issue persists, review the section on the Balance of Speed and Precision and focus on applying more of your learned skill to controlling the gun.

DRAW FROM HOLSTER EXERCISE

Drawing a snubby from a holster is another fundamental skill. When you need your snubnose, it's probably going to be in its holster, and you'll need to get it out and into a firing position quickly. As with any other shooting skill, that ability is something you need to train and practice regularly! Unless you're using a range that forbids drawing from the holster, I recommend most of your shooting practice include drawing the snubby as a first step.

This exercise is designed to develop your drawing the gun and shooting in a safe and progressive manner. Please read the section on Drawing and Reholstering for a detailed look at the techniques.

Procedure

Like the Extend-Touch-Fire exercise, Draw From Holster starts at three to four yards and you do each step of the drawstroke separately, but in sequence with a slight pause between each one. The steps (and commands) are:

GRASP — Drop into your natural shooting position as you lock your focus on the target. Get your shooting hand on the grip of the gun and into a firing grasp. If your holster has any retention devices like a thumb strap, release or defeat them as part of getting your firing grasp. Position your trigger finger so it lands on the frame of the gun, rather than the trigger, as the gun comes out of the holster.

UP — Bring the gun out of the holster and as high as is comfortable, being careful to keep the barrel parallel to your thighs. Make sure your trigger finger is on the frame of the gun, below the cylinder, as you bring the gun up.

ORIENT — Point the muzzle at the target/threat.

EXTEND, TOUCH & FIRE — As you've already practiced, extend through the ready position into your fully extended shooting position, place your finger on the trigger, and rapidly increase pressure until the shot fires. Once the shot has been fired, bring the gun back into the ready position.

RELUCTANTLY RE-HOLSTER — Slowly and carefully reverse the drawstroke to return the gun to the holster. If possible, look at the holster as you return the gun to it.

Repeat the exercise, and on each repetition speed up the process by decreasing the interval between the commands. Do this until you need to reload.

With a reloaded snubby, change the command to a single "UP!" Now smoothly put the individual steps together, eliminating the pauses and making the draw one smooth, continuous motion and firing one round per repetition. Do it slowly at first, making sure each step occurs in the proper sequence.

The re-holstering step should always have a pause between the point where you come back to the ready position and actually start to put the gun back into the holster. Again, the idea is to re-holster reluctantly!

After you've fired a full cylinder, reload and repeat but now shoot a random number of rounds, between two and four, on each repetition.

Common issues

Particularly in the early stages of learning to draw efficiently, you'll tend to "get ahead" of the steps. This is the time to build a solid draw sequence, so it's important to go through each step separately and distinctly. Make sure each step of the drawstroke is done consistently and correctly before moving on to the next step. (This is where having a training partner to keep you honest is very helpful!)

When the UP command is used, you may find yourself rushing the draw process to get faster. Speed will come with practice, so your goal at beginning is to make sure the draw is being done safely. One issue I often see is that the trigger finger finds its way inside the trigger guard as the gun comes out of the holster. Make sure your trigger finger stays in the rest position (on the frame below the cylinder) until the extension is nearly complete. A training partner or a video will be helpful to show if you're having any issues.

Pointing the muzzle at some part of the body is a common issue when re-holstering. Getting the snubby back into the holster needs to be done carefully! If possible, look at the holster to make sure nothing is occluding the opening and you're not pointing the muzzle at yourself. Just as during the draw, the barrel should remain parallel to your body as you re-holster. Also watch that your muzzle does not swing wide and cover other students or bystanders if you're at a class or public range.

Evaluation/troubleshooting

Watch for the safety issues noted above. It's too easy to become overexcited at the dynamic of drawing the gun, and then you're likely to pay less attention to the shooting skills. This will be evident if your pattern of hits changes from the Multiple Shots exercise. If so, focus on applying the skills you've learned to get the hits!

SIGHTED FIRE EXERCISE

Up to this point you've been simply focusing on the target and bringing your snubby into and parallel with your line of sight. If you've paid attention to having a proper grasp and manipulating the trigger without moving the gun, you should have been rewarded with solid hits inside the 10x10-inch (or thereabouts) target area at the most likely range of application, which is three to four yards.

Remember the discussion about when you use your sights? The answer, of course, is when you need to. In this exercise, we're going to set up conditions where you will likely need to use your sights to get accurate hits.

When you need to shoot to a greater level of precision, as when shooting a smaller or more distant target, is when you transition to using your sights. This exercise introduces you to the practice of sighted fire and utilizes a smaller target area to emphasize that the sights are used when you need them.

Review the section Using Sights for the details on how to integrate the sights into your shooting.

Procedure

1) You need a target that is considerably smaller than the upper-chest target you've been using. If you're using the Law Enforcement Targets Combat Focus Training Targets, use one of the small colored circles. If you're using my free downloadable targets, use the smallest round target. If you're making your own targets, you need one that is at least half the size of the center-chest target, and preferably in the 1/3 to 1/4 size differential. A two- to three-inch circle is ideal. Start at three to four yards.

2) On the UP command (or your decision to shoot), draw, extend on the chosen precision target area, keep your focus on the target as you align and superimpose your sights, and fire one round. If you miss, bring the gun back to the ready position, pause, then extend out on the target and again align your sights and fire one round. After you successfully make the shot, carefully and reluctantly re-holster.

3) Repeat until you've fired an entire cylinder.

4) Extend the distance: back up to five to six yards and repeat the exercise.

Common issues

It's important not to dwell on tiny details in this exercise. It's really very simple: focus on the target, align the sights, and keep them on target as you briskly increase pressure on the trigger until the gun fires. That's the whole process!

At the same time, when you need to shoot to a greater level of precision you'll find that all the fundamentals come into play. You'll likely need to focus on grasp pressure and more deliberate trigger control, which become important when shooting at smaller targets or at longer distances.

It's important to take only as much time as you need to fire the shot. It's common to "hang" on the target when you've reached extension. The more time your arms are extended before firing, the more fatigued your muscles will get and the more you'll wobble on target. When that happens, delivering accurate rounds becomes more a matter of luck than skill. Extend out, get your sights aligned, and apply increasing pressure to the trigger until the gun fires.

Another issue I often see is slowing the trigger stroke in a misguided effort to be "more careful." It's difficult to modulate the muscles in the fingers when the pressure they apply closely matches the opposing pressure of the trigger, which is exactly what happens when you slow down too much. It's good to roll the trigger back more deliberately than when you're shooting at a larger and closer target, but don't go overboard. Even when applying more control to shoot to a greater level of precision, you still need to apply enough pressure so your muscle control is maintained. The reality is that the precision trigger stroke needs to happen more quickly than most people think. It's a paradox and completely non-intuitive, but there are valid physiological reasons why moving the trigger finger a little faster usually results in better precision!

Evaluation/troubleshooting

If you're consistently shooting low (your shots hit below the target), it usually means you're trying to "grab" the trigger -- you're trying to get the shot off the instant you see the "perfect" alignment of sights on the target. The sudden muscle contraction as you try to make the shot before your sight picture changes results in your clenching not just your trigger finger, but also the other fingers. This pulls the gun down and off target. Ironically, trying for a "perfect" shot means you don't make even a "good" shot!

What can you do to reduce this tendency? First, pay attention to your grasp pressure. It's not uncommon for students to relax their grasp a bit when trying to make a single shot. Take particular care that your ring and pinkie fingers are contributing their share to your grasp.

Once you've made sure you have a proper grasp, a good cure for this problem is to do the Moving Point of Aim exercise. That exercise has proven invaluable to helping my students get past the strong desire to grab a shot.

Consistent misses in other directions usually (though not always) indicate sight alignment/sight picture issues. While you can get away with a surprising amount of sight alignment error, there are limits. The Moving Point of Aim exercise will help sort those out.

Random misses with no discernible pattern can often be traced to grasp issues. I often see students relax their grasp when they know they'll only be shooting a single round. Grasp pressure needs to be consistent whether shooting one round or ten, and paying attention to maintaining it throughout until the shot has been fired — "follow through" is the best term —often cures the issue.

"What happens if i don't really need to use my sights?"
The purpose of this drill is to help you determine when you need to use your sights. The conditions are going to be different for every person, which is why you don't see "always use your sights at this specific distance" in this book. You need to figure out for yourself when you need to use your sights, and the only way to do that is to shoot at different sized targets at different distances.

Starting with the first iteration, which is the smaller target at the distance you're already used to shooting, a lot of students can make those hits reliably without consciously using their sights. That's why the instructions include changing the distance. At some point you'll find a distance at which you can't hit that small target and are forced to use your sights. Your sights effectively extend the distance at which you can shoot at any given size of target.

If you discover you don't need to use your sights, that's fine. If you do need to use them, that's fine too. This exercise is about learning your own limitations, your own balance of speed and precision.

BALANCE OF SPEED & PRECISION EXERCISE

This exercise is the core of a good practice session and the single most important in this book. In practical terms, it combines the Multiple Shots and Sighted Fire exercises into one, but the result is more than the sum of its parts!

The BSP exercise gives you the opportunity to recognize the level of precision to which you need to shoot and to apply the skill needed to deliver accurate hits. This is how defensive shootings happen: you don't know ahead of time what level of precision will be required, and you're forced to deal with it in real time. This exercise replicates, to a small degree, the apprehension in recognition and helps you learn to recognize and recall the skills necessary, and then apply those skills to get the hits on target.

It's important to understand the concepts of the balance of speed and precision in order to get the most from this exercise. Since your balance is always affected by a host of variables, including the target size, this exercise gives you practice in rapidly changing and unpredictable requirements — the kind of experience necessary to build an understanding of your own balance under a wide range of conditions.

The range should be varied between 3 and 7 yards, with an occasional few rounds fired from as far as 10 yards. Start at the closest distances (3 to 5 yards) and work your way to the longest.

Always shoot this exercise drawing from the holster unless the range prohibits the practice. Ideally you'll have a training partner who can issue the following commands, but lacking that, you can make a virtual training partner (directions below). If nothing else, you can use a pair of dice or a shuffled deck of cards to provide the necessary randomness in the shoot commands. The random, unpredictable nature gives this exercise its tremendous value and is worth the effort to provide it.

Procedure

The two commands should be something similar to these:

- UP — This is your indication to fire multiple (but a varying number of) rounds into the chest-sized area of the target.

- A NUMBER (or LETTER or possibly COLOR, depending on the target being used) — You fire ONE round into the smaller target area denoted by that number.

The UP command should be used approximately 2/3 of the time, and the NUMBER or LETTER command the remaining 1/3. They are to be mixed up — randomized — so you cannot easily anticipate the next command. The commands are never combined. One command is given, the shooting is completed, and you re-holster to wait for the next randomized command.

This is the primary exercise in this book and should be fired at various distances between three and perhaps 10 yards. (A variant is to set up multiple targets at various distances and move among them for each repetition.) The target distances need to be realistic (plausible), so concentrate mostly on the shorter distances and only occasionally shoot at the longest.

Common issues

If you've done these exercises in order, allowing your skill to develop, you'll have had experience successfully shooting the large (chest-sized) targets with rapid, multiple shots and the smaller targets with single rounds. What you might find (and what I see with a lot of students) is that, up to this point, you've had little trouble hitting the smaller targets (usually using your sights). Then you suddenly begin missing them when doing this exercise.

Physically this is nothing more than a failure to apply the balance of speed and precision principles: as the precision increases, you need to apply more skill, which takes more time. But on a psychological basis, it's a function of processing information: you're focusing so much on figuring out what to shoot that you're no longer paying attention to how to shoot it. Over time, as your skill (and your confidence in that skill) develops, you'll need to focus less on conscious application. At this level, though, you probably need to transition quickly from processing information to consciously applying your skill to get the hits inside the area of precision the target dictates.

Evaluation/troubleshooting

If you're consistently missing the small targets, revisit the fundamentals of Grasp and Extension and the principles of Using the Sights. It's easy to overlook the application of skill when you're worried about the random shoot command.

Check that you're applying pressure to the trigger rapidly and smoothly. As discussed earlier, it's not uncommon to slow your trigger roll when faced with a more difficult shooting problem. Applying less pressure to the trigger and slowing the increase in that pressure result in every small movement of your finger causing the gun to twitch. Along with that, the total time you "hang" on target waiting for the shot to break can cause your arm muscles to tremble. Remember: while your trigger press might be slightly slower for the precision target, it should not slow to the level that fatigue becomes an issue. It sounds counterintuitive, but most of the time you'll actually shoot better if you apply pressure to the trigger a little more quickly, as long as your extension and grasp are solid.

All the other evaluation criteria in the Draw From Holster and Sighted Fire exercises are applicable to this exercise as well.

If you don't have a training partner

If you don't have the luxury of someone who can go to the range with you, it's easy to set up a substitute by making a randomized target sequence using the voice memo function on your phone.

At home, record at least five (5) voice memos with varying combinations of "UP!" and whatever designation you're using for the smaller target areas. (With the Law Enforcement Targets Combat Focus Training Targets, they're numbers. Some other targets may use letters. If you're using homemade targets, use whatever you prefer.)

The commands to shoot the smaller targets should be no more than about 30% of the total shoot commands and should be sprinkled randomly throughout the recording. A typical sequence might look like this:

UP!

UP!

UP!

3!

UP!

UP!

5!

UP!

2!

UP!

UP!

The first command should start 10 to 15 seconds into the recording, and the commands should have a varying amount of time between them to further reduce your anticipation when shooting. The intervals between commands should at the minimum be enough for you to shoot and safely re-holster before waiting for the next command.

At the range you'll need your phone, the earphones that came with it, and some shooting muffs. Insert one of the earpieces in an ear and put your muffs on. Pick one of the pre-recorded sequences at random so you don't know what's going to come up first, and start the playback. Drop your phone quickly into a pocket and wait for the first command.

ONE HAND DEFENSE EXERCISE

Shooting with both hands on the gun always gives you maximum control, both over the heavy revolver trigger and over the sharp recoil of the light, short-barreled snubby. Why, then, would you ever shoot with only one hand?

It's simple: you shoot with one hand because your other hand is busy doing something related to the incident. Your other hand may be:

- holding a child
- holding the cell phone you're using to call police
- operating a flashlight
- opening a door
- been injured by your attacker
- or any number of other things that might be important under the circumstances.

This exercise gives you a passing familiarity with drawing and shooting with your strong hand only.

One-hand shooting stance

Shooting one-handed entails a slight change to your normal two-handed shooting stance. The shoulder of your shooting arm rotates forward to bring more of your upper-body weight behind the gun, and the muscles from your upper and lower arm need to be consciously tensioned to help control recoil. The gun is kept upright (to match the orientation of your head) and is still extended into and parallel with your line of sight.

Pay particular attention to locking your elbow into the fully extended position. Unless you have an injury to the elbow, locking your arm into a straight position gives you enhanced control over the snubby's recoil forces.

Procedure

This exercise is essentially identical to the preceding exercises, except your support hand is kept busy doing something other than being on the gun. The support hand should simulate something like the examples above. For instance, if you have small children, you might mimic holding them to your chest or sweeping them behind you for cover. You can also hold your cell phone or a flashlight to your head to illuminate the target. You should also occasionally mimic an injured arm, allowing it to dangle uselessly at your side. You may think of other plausible situations requiring your other hand and simulate them on the range.

For each repetition, do something different with that hand. Rest a bit between each repetition. If you need to reload, do so with both hands — this is not a one-handed reloading exercise!

This drill is done in three progressive variants:

1) One-Hand, One Shot — Draw and fire one round to the chest area of the target, then safely re-holster. Repeat a couple of times so you get a feeling for how differently the gun reacts when held with only one hand.

2) One-Hand, Multiple Shots — draw and fire multiple rounds to the high chest area of the target, re-holstering between strings of fire. Repeat a few times.

3) One-Hand BSP: if you're doing the BSP drill, occasionally elect to shoot it one-hand only. If you have a training partner, they can randomly throw in the command "One Hand Only" before the "UP" or number/letter/color commands.

Common issues

If you've never (or seldom) shot a defensive handgun one-handed, you're going to find that the gun recoils differently. It tends to travel up in an arc toward the support side of the body. You'll also find you tire more quickly due to the increased muscle tension necessary to help control the snubby's recoil. If you're relatively new to shooting in general, this exercise is somewhat grueling. Repetitions should be done sparingly, paying close attention to your fatigue level.

As you become tired, your gun handling can suffer to the point that you do unsafe things without realizing it. Fatigued students often have safety issues with their trigger finger; it starts to stray inside the trigger guard when it shouldn't. Be sure your trigger finger goes to the trigger only during extension, and comes off the trigger as soon as you start to return to the ready position.

Pay attention to what your body is telling you! If you're getting tired, stop and rest.

Evaluation/troubleshooting

It's common to see your rounds land off to one side, which can be due to lack of sufficient grasp pressure or arm muscle tension. If shots are landing high and to the weak side in particular, that indicates the upper arm muscles are not being engaged and the shoulder is not being rolled forward sufficiently. If you looked down on yourself from above, you would want to see your shoulders slightly rotated toward the target and favoring the strong side.

If your shots are going low to the strong side, it's usually because your trigger finger is steering the gun inside your grasp. Pay closer attention to your grasp pressure and muscle tension in the lower arm.

Solid one-hand shooting stance with feigned injury to support-side arm; note increased forward roll of the shooting-arm shoulder

MOVING POINT OF AIM EXERCISE

This is one of my favorite exercises, because it helps to dispel misconceptions and solve several difficult shooting issues. The concepts here are applicable to shooting to extreme levels of precision and out to implausible distances. Properly and judiciously used, it can help you isolate and correct problems, especially if you've developed a flinch or habitually miss shots on the more precise targets (particularly if those shots are going low).

No matter how good a shooter you are, your snubby will always move no matter how precisely you aim. The difference between you and an Olympic-level competitor isn't that they hold their guns perfectly still. Their guns still move, it's just that their guns move a lot less than yours! They've learned how to control that movement to deliver the level of precision they need.

This exercise helps you come to terms with your snubby's normal movement by learning how to accept and control it enough to deliver the precision your target dictates. The target used should have a variation in area sizes, the largest being at least 3x the size of the smallest.

Procedure

You need a target with several areas of varying precision. If you don't have anything pre-printed, you can take some printer paper and draw a large (eight-inch diameter) circle on one, a medium (five-inch) circle on another, and a couple of small (two-inch) circles on the last. It's helpful to have a training partner to inject some amount of randomness in the fire command, but it's not necessary. Choose an appropriate distance that duplicates where you're having issues. If this is your first time, start at about four yards.

Round 1: This uses the largest target area you have. Start with your snubby loaded and extended on target, your finger on the trigger. On the command (or decision) MOVE, you should intentionally move the gun all over the inside of the target area. Keep the muzzle pointed inside the area's boundaries at all times, but deliberately move the gun (preferably in a random pattern) over the entire target area. At random intervals, the command UP is given (or you decide to shoot). Immediately and without stopping the gun, quickly apply pressure to the trigger to fire a single shot. Repeat this until your snubby is empty.

Round 2: Reload, move to the next smaller target area and repeat the exercise. This requires much smaller movement, and you need to remind yourself to control the gun and always keep the sights inside the target area. Fire another full cylinder of ammunition and then reload.

Round 3: Move to the first of the smallest targets and repeat the exercise.

Round 4: You'll use the other small target area, but this time you're not going to deliberately move the sights inside the target area. Instead, apply only the control necessary to keep the natural movement of the gun inside the target area. Concentrate on watching the sight movement and controlling — but not trying to stop — the movement as each shot is fired. The gun is allowed to move but in a very controlled manner. It's helpful to think, "You can move all you want, as long as you stay inside the target."

Common issues

This exercise should be used first to develop your understanding and acceptance of gun movement, and then whenever you're having problems shooting the precision target areas. At the end of the exercise, you should find the majority of your shots comfortably going into even the smallest target. If you're still missing, it's useful to repeat the exercise from the top and pay particular attention to the subtle movement of the muzzle, grasp pressure, and trigger control.

The value of this exercise diminishes rapidly as you get tired; it takes both physical ability and concentration.

Evaluation/troubleshooting

There are three reasons you may still have misses in this exercise. First, it's common to deliberately stop the gun to "grab" the shot. This is generally obvious (your shots usually jerk downward to a degree), and the solution is to remind yourself to keep the gun moving (or allow it to move). Don't try to stop the gun to make the shot!

Second, you didn't consciously keep the gun's sights inside the target area at all times. You need to control the gun to keep the sights within the target area.

Third, you didn't manipulate the trigger smoothly (which can also be a function of "grabbing the shot"). Remember to rapidly apply increasing pressure to the trigger until the shot breaks, while at the same time keeping your focus on controlling the gun's movement. This problem often results from thinking too much about the trigger and not enough about controlling the gun's movement.

This may also be a grasp issue, where the pressure applied to the trigger is enough to move the gun in your grasp. It's easy to forget fundamentals such as proper extension and grasp when concentrating on controlling the gun's movement, and this exercise helps you separate the two. It forces you to develop both the skill and confidence to ignore your well-trained trigger finger.

As long as your snub's sights stay aligned inside the target area and your trigger finger doesn't push the gun around, your shots will always hit accurately no matter when the trigger is pressed.

IMPLAUSIBLE DISTANCE EXERCISE

At the risk of repeating myself, your training and practice resources are limited. Because of this, it's impossible to be prepared for everything that could possibly happen to you. Instead, you have to make training decisions that reflect what your world looks like and how criminal attacks happen.

As I mentioned in a previous chapter, the best data we have about actual defensive shooting incidents comes from Tom Givens at Rangemaster. He found that it's uncommon to encounter shooting distances beyond 10 yards in private sector self defense. The space between about three and 10 yards is the range of probable encounters.

That doesn't mean longer shots never happen; they occasionally do. It's just that, as you get beyond the 10-yard mark, the shots become progressively less plausible. As the shooting distance approaches 25 yards, the plausibility drops dramatically.

This is all well and good, except for one thing: Most people believe the snubnose revolver is a "belly gun," a gun useful only for belly-to-belly distance encounters. It's not uncommon to hear people say that snubbies aren't capable of hitting anything beyond arm's length or that they can't be shot to high degrees of precision. Sometimes it's hard to argue against these misconceptions. The poor sights on many snubbies, along with the short sight radius (the distance between the front and rear sights) seem to validate those opinions.

For many people, then, an accurate shot beyond 10 yards with a snubnose is "impossible." This exercise is intended to give you some experience shooting your snubby at distances most people think are implausible — hence the name!

This exercise requires that you be familiar with all the concepts and exercises presented up to this point. Becoming proficient at the Moving Point of Aim exercise is particularly important, because shooting at extended distances magnifies the gun's movement (just as shooting to extreme levels of precision does). Learning to accept and control that movement is key to making accurate long-range shots.

When shooting at extended distances, everything matters. This is where you need to consciously apply all the skills you've learned!

I recommend doing this exercise sparingly to avoid wasting your precious training resources. A few times a year are sufficient.

Procedure

Set the target at 25 yards to start. This is at the edge of plausibility for private-sector defensive shootings. As you gain proficiency you can move the target back, but I suggest that 50 yards be the limit — not because you can't make longer shots with a snubby, but because doing so isn't a wise use of your training and practice resources.

The target should resemble the Combat Focus Training Target: you need a chest-sized target area, preferably surrounded by a recognizable torso to help you gauge your sight placement when you can't clearly see an aiming point. The space around the target area will show any misses, which helps isolate and correct shooting issues.

Round One: Start with the snubby in the ready position and in your shooting stance. Extend onto the target, align your sights and place them on target. Allow the gun to settle down until your sights are moving within the target area — but not outside of it. When that happens, apply increasing pressure to the trigger until the shot fires. Come back to the ready position. Repeat until you've fired a full cylinder, then reload. Holster your snubby and check your target. If less than 50% of your hits are inside the target area (or any of your shots are completely off the target), repeat while paying closer attention to the fundamentals of stance, sight alignment and placement, and trigger control.

Round Two: Since this is a defensive shooting exercise, practice this from a holstered condition. On the command (or decision) to shoot, rapidly draw your snubby, get into your stable shooting stance, extend and fire one round. Repeat for the full cylinder before checking your hits.

Round Three: This is the same as Round Two, except your goal is to decrease the time it takes between the command or decision to shoot and the point at which the shot breaks. The keys here are to move fast and shoot carefully — get the gun out of the holster, with a solid two-hand grasp, and extend onto the target without delay. Allow the sights to settle at the same time you start to apply pressure to the trigger.

Common issues

The most common problem I see is a lack of belief that it can be done at all! So many people believe the snubnose cannot be shot at anything beyond "bad breath" distance that many students start with a strong idea that it can't be done. Rest assured that your snubnose is mechanically capable of landing accurate shots at that distance. There is nothing deficient in the gun's capabilities. The challenges are working with the bad sights and short sight radius and getting past your own doubts.

Most technique issues are the same as in the previous exercises. Pay conscious attention to applying the skill you have. When the distance increases, all the little things add up to hits (or misses!).

Evaluation/troubleshooting

There's not much here that previous exercises haven't already revealed. If you've conscientiously developed your skills in the earlier exercises (and applied them), most of the common problems will have already been sorted out.

One issue that might not have shown up in earlier exercises is the regulation (adjustment) of the gun's sights. Since the vast majority of snubnose revolvers have fixed sights, they're regulated at the factory to theoretically hit to point of aim. Some companies are better at this task than others, but even the best companies fail occasionally. Colt Detective Special revolvers from the 1980s, for instance, are notorious for hitting high and to the left — an issue that often goes unnoticed until the distance gets extended a bit. If your shots are landing in a definable and consistent group that is outside the target area, that's usually a sign your sights are not regulated properly. If that group of shots is landing to the left or right, the fix usually requires taking the snubby to a reputable gunsmith and having the sights adjusted.

If the group is well defined and consistent but either high or low, it might be that the ammunition you're using isn't what the sights were regulated for.

Changing the bullet weight and/or velocity often brings those shots back onto the target.

What if you don't have a discernible and consistent group? If you miss the target area but your shots don't have a discernible pattern, if what you're seeing is a general increase in the dispersion of your shots, that's usually a sign that you need to apply more control over the gun's movement inside the target area. You may need to use that psychological trick from the Moving Point of Aim exercise: think, "You can move all you want, as long as you stay inside this area."

Once your sights are moving inside the target area, apply increasing pressure to the trigger. Waiting for the sights to settle more than that simply increases your fatigue level and makes it more difficult to fire an accurate shot.

Also pay close attention to your trigger manipulation. Again, the slower your trigger roll, the more likely it is that you'll increase the muzzle deviation and therefore miss the shot. Your trigger finger should be slow enough to allow you to keep the sights inside the target area, but not so slow that it stutters during trigger travel. That balance is probably the hardest part to master.

THE IMPORTANCE OF A TRAINING PARTNER

When you go to the range to practice your defensive shooting skills, do you usually go by yourself? If you're like most of my students, you do. I'd like you to consider taking a training partner with you, because he or she can dramatically improve the quality of your defensive snubnose practice!

Think for a minute why you carry your snubnose revolver, and why you train and practice with it: to prepare yourself to deal with a lethal attack you didn't know was going to happen. (If you knew it was going to happen, you'd probably choose to avoid it altogether!) You should be training to deal with what we call an ambush attack: the one you didn't recognize until it was actually underway.

Contrast that with the way you probably practice: you know what you're going to shoot, you know where it is, you know where it needs to be shot, and you know how many times you're going to shoot it. You also have plenty of time to work yourself into a position where you can shoot efficiently.

What's missing? Training the response when you didn't know it was going to happen!

That missing element of surprise — even if it's just a little surprise — is what divorces your practice from reality. Think about your daily life: you're sitting in a restaurant with your lovely date, alternating between staring into each other's eyes and eyeing the menu. At that moment, are you even thinking (let alone preparing) for the guy who bursts into the restaurant with a shotgun? How prepared were you, at that moment, to shoot someone else to save your life (and that of your date)?

You need a way to link what you're doing on the range to how you're likely to use those skills when you actually need them. What you need to do is build the mental link between your recognition of the need to shoot and your recall of the skills necessary to shoot rapid, multiple, accurate rounds.

The recognition part is hard to do when you're by yourself, because — again — you know all that information ahead of time. It's difficult to build that important recognition-recall link if you never have anything you need to recognize!

Building recognition into training

In order to have something to recognize, you need to reduce (as much as you possibly can) your anticipation of the need to shoot, to get rid of the preplanning you do for every shot when you're alone. Outside of controlled force-on-force training exercises, the best way to do that is to introduce randomness into your training.

By "randomness," I mean reducing or eliminating the ability to predict the need to shoot by forcing you to process information and act on that information prior to shooting. It's difficult to do on your own, but a training partner makes it easy!

Provide your training partner with multiple target options (some of which should be "don't shoot" in some manner), and allow him to decide what you'll be doing next. He then presents you with a start command that forces you to think about what he said (process information) and from that figure out what you need to shoot (if anything). He can present the available choices randomly and in ways that are hard to predict. His job is to reduce your anticipation and therefore your ability to pre-plan what you're going to do.

All it takes is a little imagination, and perhaps a little mischievousness on his part. His job, quite literally, is to try to confuse you!

The partner's job

In each of the exercises, I've listed suggested commands your partner can use. As you both get more comfortable with the exercises, your partner should be encouraged to deviate and come up with new ways to force you to think before you shoot.

For instance, if your targets have numbers, he can give you a math problem you have to solve "on the fly," the solution giving you the target you need to shoot. If the targets have letters, he can use first or last letters of words to indicate the target. He can combine letters, numbers, and colors; ask questions about current events; and anything else that messes with your mind and gets you to focus on thinking about something other than pulling the trigger. He gets to play with your mind by throwing you off your mental balance and into an environment where you have to make decisions based on the information he gives you, rather than simply regurgitating a choreographed response.

Yes, it works. The first time you use a partner, you'll probably find that your shooting skills have magically deteriorated. I've had students with thousands of hours of high-level training fall apart the first time they were forced into this kind of induced randomness, simply because they were used to predictable and staged exercises.

Getting pushed out of your comfort zone and given the opportunity to fail are parts of the learning process — and have the advantage of being more like "real life" than all but the most elaborate and expensive scenario training systems.

The best part? If he's a shooter too, you'll get your chance to do it to him!

What qualifications does your training partner need?

If you got the idea that your training partner doesn't need to be a shooter, or even know much about shooting, you're right. His job isn't to coach you or point out your shooting flaws (though it's great if he can), but rather to think several steps ahead of you.

All you need to do is acquaint him with the exercise being done, what the objectives and options are, and how he can randomize his commands. Then let him do his job while you concentrate on processing the information he's feeding you.

OPTIONS FOR RESTRICTED RANGES

Those of us who live in the defensive training world can sometimes forget that we're fortunate. We usually have the use of ranges that permit a wide range of realistic training movements, sometimes being allowed to do things the average user wouldn't be allowed to do. That privilege can lead to an elitist point of view, particularly if we formulate our instruction in such a way that the average person can't possibly follow it.

In most cases, the shooting range you have available will likely have some restrictions. For instance, many ranges prohibit drawing from the holster. Others prohibit any sort of movement, and a large percentage prohibit "rapid fire" (usually defined as more than one round per second). Just recently I was forced to teach on a range that not only had all of those restrictions, but also restricted the placement of handgun targets at a fixed 25 feet from the shooters!

Find another range

My first recommendation is always to search for a better range, one that will allow you to practice your skills in the ways you are likely to use them. That means drawing from a holster and firing rapid multiple shots at variable distances to the target. It's worth driving some distance to find a range like that. If the choice is a 15-minute drive to a restricted range or an hour's drive to a better range, I suggest making that long drive — even if it means you practice less often. In my opinion, less frequent but more relevant and realistic practice beats more frequent but unrealistic practice every time.

Sometimes finding a suitable range means heading to a gravel pit or hillside on public lands "in the sticks." While I'm less enamored of this option and wouldn't choose it if there were any alternatives, in some locales it may be the only way to train realistically. If that's what you have available, by all means consider it — but first exhaust all your other options. (Never, under any circumstances, go alone. Being out in the woods by yourself and with valuable firearms is not the safest course of action.)

Jump through the hoops

Many ranges, particularly those run by gun clubs, permit a greater variety of activities for their members. One club I know of reserves the use of "unrestricted" ranges, those where anything is allowed as long as it's safe, to members only. The general public can only use the ranges with very severe limitations.

Becoming a member in a gun club gets you past those kinds of restrictions. On the downside, club dues can be steep and you'll need to deal with the inevitable club politics. But when you factor in the freedom you'll have and the money you'll save on commercial range fees, you might find it's worth the investment.

Other ranges and clubs may do something similar with regard to shooting organizations. Many ranges, for instance, only allow members of groups such as the International Defensive Pistol Association (IDPA) or United States Practical Shooting Association (USPSA) to draw from holsters and shoot rapid fire. Some of the best ranges are run by clubs associated with those groups, and it's often worth the effort to join just to have access to their facilities.

It's not unusual to find ranges that allow unrestricted use only if you've taken one of their in-house classes. Sometimes they are merely safety briefings, though they may be a beginner's shooting or self-defense course. This is often true with commercial (for-profit) shooting ranges. One in my area has an unrestricted "tactical" range that they reserve for police officers and people who've been through one of their classes. Again, I think it's worth the investment (and aggravation) in order to train realistically. Plus, sometimes that access comes with a "members' only" deal on range fees and/or ammunition!

Finally, you'll occasionally find ranges that require you to pass some sort of shooting test to be let out from under their onerous restrictions. In some cases these tests are simply to see that you can, in fact, handle your firearm without hurting yourself or others. But sometimes you have to pass arbitrary "standards" designed to enforce the purity of the user group; it's more of a way to maintain a clique than actually promoting safety or competency. While those tests can be annoying or even demeaning, keep the end goal in mind: the ability to practice more frequently and more realistically. I think it's worth a little pain to do that.

When all else fails, adapt

Lots of people live in areas, particularly urban areas, where none of those options are available. It's either accept restrictions or don't shoot. Even under those conditions, you can get in some useful practice.

When drawing from the holster is not allowed

This is perhaps the most common restriction for indoor ranges. In some ways it's understandable: next time you're at an indoor range, look up at the ceiling. You'll probably see angled baffles, made of steel and often covered with acoustic tile, with many marks left from bullet impacts. Lots of people unfortunately try to play "fast draw" like they see in the movies and end up putting a bullet into the baffles. If not for those devices, the bullets would be exiting the roof! Were you the range owner or operator (or their insurance company), you'd probably prohibit drawing from the holster too.

For us, however, it's a definite crimp in our ability to practice realistically. But you can get some good defensive shooting practice in by remembering that the draw just gets the gun into something resembling the ready position. You can still practice from the ready position, as in the Extend-Touch-Fire exercise, and essentially practice half of the drawstroke. If you want to make it a little more consistent with how the gun comes out of the holster, you can start just before the ready portion of the drawstroke: with the gun at your side, as it would be on the "Orient" step of the draw. From there, extend through the ready position and shoot.

Quick-access practice: You can do some practice to simulate using your snubby in a home or family defense role. In the section on Safe and Ready Storage, I talked about the quick-access safes that can keep unauthorized users away from your snubnose, yet leave it ready for you to retrieve in an emergency. Even ranges that don't allow drawing from the holster usually have nothing to say about having a gun box on the counter in front of you!

For most of the exercises in this book, you can bring your quick-access safe and practice retrieving and loading your snubby to deal with a simulated threat. This gives you great practice in a task that you need to know how to do if you choose that storage method. It's also a skill that most people neglect to practice. Even if they've been to a number of shooting classes and can draw their gun quickly, the act of retrieving it from storage for immediate response is usually one they're relatively unfamiliar with. The restricted range can be your chance to get a leg up on this important skill.

If your safe is securely bolted to the floor or wall, you obviously can't take it to the range with you. You can always buy a second quick-access safe, though that's an expensive proposition. Instead, you can use any rigid, latching box as a stand-in for the safe. Many gun cases will fill that role admirably. If you don't have one, your local gun or outdoor store no doubt has many from which to choose. You can even use a common military surplus ammunition can!

Simply put the box or case on the counter in front of you, and on a command (or your decision) get into the box, retrieve your snubby, load it, then extend through the ready position and shoot. Come back to the ready position and pause for a bit; if you need to reload to continue the exercise, do so. When you're finished, put the snubby down for about a minute (to mentally separate the simulation from the administrative tasks), unload it and put it back into the "safe" for the next round.

I meet many people who don't have concealed carry licenses or choose not to carry a gun on their person, instead using the gun solely as a home defense tool, and for them this is a vital drill.

When rapid fire is not allowed

To me, this is perhaps the most galling restriction because it's usually not a safety issue. The "no rapid fire" rules generally stem from old-fashioned target shooting ranges, where people feel their concentration is thrown off by the sound of a string of shots next to them. While I certainly espouse being a polite range user (see the section on Range Etiquette), the fact is that practicing realistic defensive shooting skills requires us to shoot rapid, multiple, accurate rounds on target. It's hard to develop that skill if you're restricted to one round every second!

The great importance of shooting a string of fire is learning to control recoil properly. If you're only firing one shot, you'll have a tendency to relax because you know you don't need to maintain control over the gun for an immediate second (or third or fourth) round. No matter how dedicated you are to maintaining follow-through, eventually you'll succumb to the natural tendency to relax because "it's just one round."

So, your first job is to consciously think "follow-through" for each and every round you fire on the restricted range. It's critical to maintain your concentration on the threat, and your optimal grasp pressure, for that long space between shots. (If you don't think a second is a long time to hold a heavy object at arm's length while squeezing your hand muscles, try it!) This is why I recommend you shoot a few rounds, then put the snubby down and relax for a minute before doing it again. (Looking at the bright side, this will definitely develop your arm and hand muscles!)

Another thing you can do is practice landing accurate first-round hits as rapidly as possible. Remember that the first round is your best opportunity to affect your attacker's ability to hurt you, because after that first round, people have a tendency to start moving. Your subsequent shots might be harder to land accurately, hence my insistence on first-shot accuracy.

Since a limitation of one round per second effectively makes every shot a first shot, take advantage of that. Come back to the ready position after each shot, and practice extending, touching the trigger, and firing an accurate round as quickly as possible. After a while, you'll probably find that your ability to make a very rapid first-round shot, and have the bullet hit accurately, has increased.

If you're limited to slow rates of fire anyhow, you can also practice making rapid but accurate shots on the smaller precision targets. As I mentioned in the Moving Point of Aim exercise, learning and accepting your "wobble zone" is critical to making accurate shots on precision targets (or targets at a longer distance). Practicing single shots on a restricted range, with the objective of making accurate shots happen faster, forces you to accept and control your sight's "wobble" more quickly than you normally would.

When the targets are placed at an unrealistic distance
As noted, I recently had to teach a course on a range where the target distance was at the long edge of likelihood for defensive shooting purposes — and the range operators wouldn't budge on their restrictions!

As discussed in the section on the Balance of Speed and Precision, the more control you need to exert over your snubby, such as when dealing with smaller or more distant targets, the more slowly you'll shoot as a consequence. Shooting at, say, 25 feet is certainly within the realm of plausibility, but shooting at that distance all the time doesn't allow you to experience the dynamics of shooting at more likely distances. It also makes learning to shoot on very precise targets significantly more difficult, at least in the beginning stages of your development.

Being forced to shoot at longer distances is a perfect chance to practice use of your snubby's sights. Remember when you use your sights? When you need to! For most people under most conditions, 25 feet is a distance where the sights will be needed. Practice keeping your focus on the threat (target) and super-imposing your blurry-but-aligned sights over the top to make the hits. Use the large (upper-chest-sized) target area for most of this shooting, perhaps using the smaller precision targets for a few rounds once you've mastered the rapid use of your sights.

This is another good chance to practice your ability to get a rapid first-round hit. Because you'll be forced to use your sights, it's a perfect opportunity to get used to the concepts introduced in the Moving Point of Aim exercise. Once you're comfortable with that, your hits on the small targets, even at an extended distance, become far more likely. Is shooting to such high levels of precision at that distance really a plausible skill? It's a stretch, I admit, but a few rounds learning what you really can and cannot do at that distance is an important part of learning your balance of speed and precision.

I caution that shooting constantly at distance targets does nothing for your ability to shoot faster at closer ranges. Though I could probably get much argument from my colleagues in the training world, in my estimation this restriction is the most damaging to your ability to develop realistic defensive shooting skills. Avoid ranges with this restriction as much as you possibly can.

DRY PRACTICE

Some people approach dry-fire (pulling the trigger with no ammunition in the gun) with almost religious enthusiasm. Some even say dry-fire is the most important thing you can do to develop your defensive shooting skills. Personally, I've not found that to be the case at all. In a strictly athletic sense, my best progression has been through carefully controlled dry-fire immediately prior to live fire. That process provides mental linkage between the skills that are practiced and their effect with live ammunition. Whether that athletic progression has resulted in my being better able to defend myself with a firearm is open to debate!

But dry practice has a definite value: the manipulation of the snubnose up to and including a simulated "shot" on an empty chamber. Being able to work out issues with stance, extension, drawing from the holster, and more in the comfort of your own home and on your own schedule can be extremely valuable. That is, as long as you understand the limitations as well as the potential benefits!

Safety first!

Dry practice can be dangerous if you don't pay attention to safety consciously and constantly.

Set up your space

The space you use for dry practice should be "sterilized" — that is, completely purged of any and all ammunition. For that reason, always do your dry practice in a space that can be separated from other areas of your house. Any place that has a door will be suitable, and the key is to keep all ammunition on the other side of the door! A room where you store your ammunition, or in which you do any handloading, is a poor choice. Your dry-fire space truly should be sterile, devoid of any ammunition.

The ideal practice space would have ballistically safe walls all the way around so there is more than one generally safe direction; a basement room is ideal. Not all of us are so fortunate, however, and must make do. If you don't have a basement (or don't live in a split-level home), you'll need to provide a ballistically safe target at which to aim your snubby. A case of printer paper, with the reams stacked in such a way that you're always aiming at the paper face rather than the edges, will easily capture any handgun (and even most rifle) bullets. That will be your safe backstop and the place where you'll hang your dry practice target.

If you do have a basement, you'll have more flexibility with placement. If you have an appropriate wall, you may even be able to hang the same full-sized target you use at the range. What is behind your target must have the ability to stop any bullet that could inadvertently be fired from your snubby. (Remember the third safety rule?)

Speaking of targets, you should always use a specific practice target and it should always be in the same place. Some people do their dry practice on whatever is in the room: a television, light switch, bathtub faucet (don't laugh, I've seen pictorial evidence) and just about anything else you can imagine. This is not a safe practice, because those aren't designed to stop a bullet. The possibility, however slim, exists that you could accidentally pull the trigger on a loaded chamber.

These procedures — establishing a sterile area, using a solid backstop, and being consistent in what you use as a target — are designed to reduce to the very lowest degree the chance of an accident. But there is always a non-zero risk, and ignoring any of these procedures will raise your risk of an accident. Be specific and consistent!

Before you do any dry practice, double-check that space to make sure no live ammunition is present anywhere. When you start your practice routine, unload your snubby outside your sterile area. Put the ammunition in a secure place and go into your practice room with that verified empty gun. Make sure your pockets are empty, too!

What and how to dry practice

Dry practice can help you develop specific skills and habits. The following skills can be done in, and benefit from, dry practice:

- Ready Position
- Grasp
- Stance
- Extension
- Trigger Control
- Drawing and Re-holstering

You can also do some of the exercises to help you apply those skills:

- Grasp Pressure
- Extend-Touch-Fire
- Draw From Holster
- One-Hand Defense
- Moving Point of Aim

The key to successful dry practice is a focus on performing and applying the skills properly. Dry practice is the perfect opportunity to slow down and make sure you understand each part of each skill.

For instance, if you're doing the Extend-Touch-Fire exercise, this is the time to slow the extension and make sure you touch the trigger as you reach the limit of extension, not before. It's also a good chance to check that your gun is coming up into your line of sight immediately, then extending straight out to the target — and that the muzzle is neither "bowling" nor "flycasting."

Dry practice is also a good time to video yourself doing each exercise or practicing each skill. You'll be surprised what video can reveal! Even performing skills in a mirror, as some advocate, doesn't reveal the problems that a 10-second video will. I heartily encourage you to take advantage of the technology built into almost every cell phone these days, because it can help fill the gaps in your own fallible observation. It's not perfect, and it's not a substitute for expert help, but it can help fix obvious issues.

Dry practice relieves the anxiety (or the excitement) of the shot and makes it possible to focus consciously on the skill or manipulation. It also builds your ability to follow through after the simulated act of firing. Dry practice can be extremely useful, but only if you do it conscientiously!

Limitations of dry practice

Nothing is perfect, however, and dry practice has some limitations you should be aware of.

The primary issue with all dry practice where the trigger is manipulated (a dry shot "fired") is the lack of accountability for the accuracy of the shot. Because no bullet is exiting the muzzle, there is no hit on the target to evaluate, and so you don't really know if you were "successful." That's why the caveat above about target evaluation, because there is no target to evaluate!

As you gain experience, you'll find that the correlation between what you do in dry practice and what you do in live fire increases, but it's never 100%. After all, if you could do everything in dry practice, there would never be a reason to go to the range.

Another limitation has to do with multiple shots. Because there is no ammunition fired and therefore no recoil, there is zero benefit to pulling the trigger more than once on any repetition. A huge part of defensive shooting is the skill to fire rapid, multiple, accurate rounds on target, and most of the skill lies in your ability to manage the recoil of your snubby. Dry practice affords you no opportunity to do that. To develop the critical skill of controlling the snubnose revolver in a realistic string of defensive fire, you need to go to the shooting range.

A big problem, and in many ways related to the lack of recoil, is the tendency to get lazy in your application of skill. This is the same problem I see on the live-fire range when people shoot only one round, or do exercises where they repetitively shoot the same number of rounds all the time. They relax because they know there won't be another shot they need to control.

The same thing can happen in dry practice; because you know there won't be any recoil to control, you relax. Grasp pressure is reduced, stance becomes a little lazier, extension isn't as complete, and muscle control in the shoulders and arms is lessened.

Fighting your own laziness — the tendency to cheat the exercise — is the biggest problem you'll face in dry practice. You have to consistently police yourself to ensure you're doing everything just as you would if you knew a bullet was coming out of your snubby's muzzle!

Finally, without the accountability a shot gives you, it's hard to build a solid correlation between what you think you can do and what you actually can. It's easy to be really "good" at dry practice but not be able to hit the target reliably in live fire. It's very easy to come out of a dry practice session with the impression that you're better than you really are. When you get to the live-fire range, you might find yourself shooting faster than you can really get accurate hits. Not all your shots will be accurate, which is a waste of the time, energy, and ammunition you've just expended.

Similar to policing your own laziness, you need to control your ego after a dry practice session. Re-calibrate your belief in your abilities by going to the live-fire range and looking at your targets.

Dry practice isn't an evaluation tool; it's a practice environment. Don't let yourself believe it's a predictor of success, either at the shooting range or against an actual attacker. It's a way to help you develop and hone some physical skills, nothing more.

MODIFYING FOR BETTER FUNCTION

While the snubnose revolver is a great self-defense tool, it isn't perfect! Many snubnose revolvers benefit from some small modifications to improve their function or to make them easier for you to use. Some modifications can be done at home by anyone with a bit of manual dexterity, while others require the services of a skilled gunsmith.

These modifications are all worthwhile to varying degrees, and most of my snubbies have had some made. Of the myriad things you can do to a snubby, these are the modifications I've found most useful.

Changing grips

The first thing you can do to make your snubby easier to shoot is fit it to your hands. The great thing about snubbies is that it's easy to change out the grips! If your hands are relatively small, you can probably find grips that will decrease the distance from the back to the trigger and make it easier to achieve proper trigger-finger placement.

If you have large hands and find your snubby a little cramped, you can likewise install larger grips. They can increase the reach to the trigger if you have long fingers, and change the circumference of the grip to increase the area the hand contacts. If you have very meaty hands, you can find grips that protrude below the grip frame and give you a little more grasping room.

Some grips can provide increased traction and enhanced recoil control. Soft, tacky rubber grips are very popular with target shooters because they seem to stick to the hands better. But they have a downside for concealed carriers: They grab your clothing just as well as they grab your hands. They can snag a cover garment and reveal the presence of the concealed gun, or they can slow the draw significantly (particularly if the gun is carried in a confined space like a pocket). For those reasons, I much prefer grips without extreme stickiness.

Grips don't have to be sticky to improve your control. Another way to get increased traction is by roughening the surface of the grip material. The traditional method is checkered wood, a staple of snubbies to this day. You can find many varieties of checkered wood grips, from large grip companies to small one-man custom grip shops. Many people feel a set of custom wood grips is an ideal complement to blued steel. They go out of their way to acquire particularly outstanding pieces of decorative wood and have them fashioned into grips that fit their hands perfectly.

The modern equivalents of checkered wood are the various textured laminates and polymers, such as the G10 grips made by companies like VZ Grips. These new-age materials are available in a wide range of colors, and though not traditional, they can really dress up a snubby!

Filling in behind the trigger guard

One thing to look for in snubnose grips is that they fill in the gap behind the trigger guard. If you look at a snubby from the side, behind the trigger guard is a cut in the frame where your fingers are intended to be. The issue with most snubbies is that cut is so much deeper than it needs to be, and the grip frame behind the cut is so narrow, that there is very little to no contact between your middle finger and the frame. Many factory grips, particularly those on older snubbies, leave that gap open.

This results in a loss of control and, in some cases, pain from the trigger guard impacting the middle finger. The Colt Agent and Cobra revolvers, for instance, are lightweight alloy versions of the famed Colt Detective Special. I once had an Agent with the original factory grips, which were made of very nice walnut and beautifully checkered. Like almost all the factory grip designs of that era they left the gap unfilled. Because my middle finger had nothing to grasp, the gun wobbled in my hands no matter how hard I squeezed!

The first round I fired drove the back of the trigger guard into the knuckle of my middle finger. It was intensely painful, and I didn't shoot that gun again until I'd put on a pair of grips that properly filled in the gap. After that modification, the little Agent became a trusted carry companion.

A proper grip design fills in the gap behind the trigger guard so the gun rides on top of your middle finger and gives enough material to properly grasp.

Every grip designer has a slightly different view of just how deep and of what shape the finger cut-out needs to be, so it is helpful to try several to find which fits your hand comfortably.

Since very few gun stores today stock a wide variety of snubby grips (if they have any at all), a good place to find them is at a large gun show. Look for examples of your snubby model that sport grips different than what you have and check them for fit. You'll no doubt find something that suits you, and you can then look for a similar set to fit yours.

(Tip: Check the boxes of grips that often sit under the tables. Revolver grips aren't in demand these days, and I rarely find a gun show that doesn't have at least one big box filled with grips at bargain prices.)

This caveat to filling in the gap does not apply to modern Ruger revolvers such as the GP100 and SP101, whose frames are designed without that exaggerated gap. The stock Ruger grips are generally fine for most hands, although people with even small-sized hands often find the stock SP101 grips too small in circumference. There are many options for the SP101, and I've found that the Pachmayr Compac grip for that gun fits a wide variety of hand sizes.

Finger grooves

Many people feel that having a grip with finger grooves cut into the front increases their control over the gun. As a result, many grip styles feature finger grooves. I'm not a fan of the concept, for several reasons.

First, in order to be useful, the finger grooves have to precisely fit your hand. If your fingers are thinner or fatter than the model around whose hand the grips were fashioned, you won't get the full benefit of the grooves. If your fingers are thinner, they'll be spread apart as you grasp the gun, which doesn't allow the fingers to work together as a unit to apply the greatest amount of pressure.

You may even find that recoil is channeled into a specific finger because of its peculiar contact with the ridge between the grooves, painfully amplifying perceived recoil rather than reducing it. This is a downside I've personally experienced!

If your fingers are larger than the grooves, part of your flesh will sit on top of the ridges and the gun's recoil will drive that ridge into your flesh — which, again, can be painful and reduce your control over the snubby.

Even if your fingers are perfectly sized to the dimensions of the finger grooves, you may not get a perfect grasp on the gun as you draw it from the holster. No one gets a perfect grasp every time; even legendary revolver shooter Jerry Miculek says he doesn't! With finger grooves and ridges, that imperfect grasp may result in a significant loss of control because your fingers can't get solid and even contact with the grip.

That's why I recommend staying away from finger groove grips. Look instead for grips that have a plain front surface but fill your hand and allow you a complete firing grasp with all your fingers in contact with each other. You'll get maximum control, maximum comfort, and maximum usability!

Fixing the trigger

The most common complaint about snubnose revolvers probably has to do with the weight of the trigger. In today's market, a typical factory-fresh snubnose trigger requires around 12 pounds of force to operate. That's a lot; in comparison, the average striker-fired semiauto pistol requires less than half of that to fire. What's more, that force has to be applied over a much greater distance than that of the autoloading pistol. No wonder the snubby is considered challenging to shoot!

Many people modify their triggers to reduce the amount of force required to operate. This can be easily done by changing out two springs inside the gun for some of lighter weight. A handy person can do this themselves at home, though many prefer to let a gunsmith handle that chore. One spring powers the hammer, and the other spring powers the trigger reset.

The biggest caveat with changing out the hammer spring is that doing so can compromise reliability. A lighter hammer spring, though making the trigger easier to operate, reduces the force with which the hammer hits the primer on the cartridge. This can result in misfires — definitely something you don't want in a defensive firearm!

Any spring changes should be followed by extensive live-fire testing to verify proper ignition, along with visual examination of the fired rounds to make sure the primer indentations are sufficient.

The spring that resets the trigger is called the rebound spring. A too-light rebound spring can cause the trigger to stick in the rearmost (fired) position, rather than return properly. A lightened rebound spring needs to reset the trigger reliably every time, with some margin for error as the gun gets dirty or the lubricants age.

Most spring kits have a selection of spring rates for both the hammer and rebound springs, so the gun can be tuned for maximum reliability with the best reduction in trigger weight. It's a balancing act and should only be attempted with proper testing afterward.

Weight isn't everything

Reducing the amount of force the trigger requires is only part of making a snubby easier to shoot. A snubby that has a smooth trigger travel without noticeable stuttering, "grittiness," or change in effort, is often easier to shoot than one that is numerically lighter but less smooth.

Smoothing out the trigger travel is a job for a gunsmith. The snubby is disassembled and the operating surfaces of all parts are smoothed. The tool marks from the machining at the factory are taken out and the surfaces polished to a mirror finish. Once reassembled and properly lubricated, the effect can be dramatic. The trigger becomes smoother and far easier to manipulate and, even without a change in springs, the reduction in friction usually results in the trigger weight dropping by a couple of pounds.

Another benefit of having the trigger fixed by a skilled revolver gunsmith is a change in the nature of the trigger travel. In most snubbies, the trigger weight over its travel isn't linear. It may be higher at the start than at the end, or higher just before the hammer falls than when the trigger started moving. Some triggers (particularly those of Smith & Wesson J-Frame snubbies) start light, get much heavier in the middle, then suddenly get very light just before the hammer is released. That odd "hump" in the trigger travel makes them the most challenging snubbies to shoot!

A good revolver gunsmith can alter the interior parts to make the trigger effort more linear: the same weight all through the trigger's travel, which makes the gun much easier to shoot.

The trigger face

Another trigger-related modification is to change the face of the trigger itself. Most modern snubbies come with triggers that have rounded, smooth faces — an ideal combination for double-action shooting. But not all snubbies are so equipped, and in the past many of them came with wide triggers or triggers that had a series of fine grooves machined into their face.

Those triggers were designed like the triggers on target-shooting revolvers, where the gun was cocked and the pad of the trigger finger placed gently on the trigger's surface. Double-action defensive shooting bears no resemblance to that! A good double-action trigger needs to be smooth, rounded, and narrow so the trigger finger can properly slide over its face as the trigger and trigger finger move back together.

If your snubby has one of those wide or grooved triggers, rounding the edges and getting rid of the grooves will greatly improve your double-action shooting. In fact, for many people that one modification is sufficient to cure their shooting problems.

Sight enhancements

A common complaint about snubnose revolvers has to do with the often poor fixed sights. A very few snubbies, most notably the Ruger SP101 and the Pro Series from Smith & Wesson, have fairly decent fixed sights, while an even smaller number have decent adjustable sights. Most of the sights on snubbies, though, leave quite a bit to be desired.

The front blade is often simply a plain ramp that tends to disappear against a similarly colored target. This is particularly true if the direction of the light illuminates the ramp evenly. If your snubby's front blade is pinned onto the barrel or is held on with a dovetail joint, replacing it with something more visible is easy (you may even be able to do it yourself, depending on how adventurous you are).

Many different sights are available to fit many of the popular snubbies, and your gunsmith can advise you on what's available for your gun.

If your front blade isn't held in with a pin or dovetail it was probably machined as part of the barrel. In that case, it's still possible to have a gunsmith modify the blade to make it more visible. Common modifications include a gold bead (the classic revolver sight), a fiber-optic insert that glows in available light, or a red or yellow plastic insert that gives a nice contrasting color to make the blade stand out.

In some cases, your gunsmith can machine away an integral front sight and cut a groove or dovetail to accept a common pinned or dovetail sight. This will give you access to a wider variety of front blades and make it easier to get just the right front sight.

The "poor man's" solution to disappearing front sights is the application of a durable bright paint to the visible part of the blade. Many people have used fingernail polish in the appropriate shade to make their front sights easier to see. Though it wear offs after a time, it's surprisingly durable and easily reapplied. You can also use model paint, the kind that's sold in tiny bottles at craft stores.

Specialized sight paint kits are available at gun stores, but I've found them no more durable than the alternatives already mentioned. They do have the advantage of being available in purer and brighter colors than nail polish, but in my experience they haven't been as durable.

Whether nail polish, model paint, or specialized sight paint, you'll get the best results on a black or blued sight blade if you first apply a white base or primer coat. Without that base coat, the darker shade shows through the color, and the result is much darker than you might anticipate.

The thin-blade S&W problem

The worst snubby sights are probably those found on some of the older Smith & Wesson J-Frames, most notably the Model 36 and Model 38, which for a time came with a very thin front blade. A typical front sight is around 1/8-inch (.125-inch) wide, but the thin-blade models were approximately half that width. Even a person with good eyes and sharply focused on the front sight often couldn't see them.

As if that weren't bad enough, because they were machined as one piece with the rest of the barrel, they had the same finish as the rest of the gun. The blued models weren't so bad, but when the gun was nickel-plated, the sight was plated too. That bright front sight disappeared under almost any lighting conditions.

Because the sights and barrels were one piece, the only way to change out the sight was to machine the old one off and find a way to attach a new blade. On most snubbies, that wouldn't be a problem, but these models also had narrow barrels with thin walls, which limited the amount of machining that could be done. The only way to fix the problem was to weld a new blade onto the barrel, which (aside from the machine and fabrication costs) entailed refinishing. If I had one of those guns, rather than trying to fix the problem, I'd just buy a different snubby!

Regulating to point of aim

It's not uncommon to find a snubby that doesn't shoot where the fixed sights are pointed. A gunsmith can often fix that problem by regulating the sights to your specific needs.

If the gun is shooting to the left or right of point of aim, the gunsmith can turn the barrel in the frame to correct the problem. The post-1972 Colt Detective Special snubby is known for this problem; in fact, it's rare to see a factory original example that doesn't shoot off to one side. It's an easy fix as long as the gunsmith has the proper barrel blocks and frame wrench. Ask to be sure!

A snubby that shoots low is regulated by carefully machining or filing a bit off the top of the front sight, which brings the barrel up in the sight picture and corrects the problem. You can even do this at home, but be careful: it only takes a bit, and it's best to file a little and then test-fire as you go.

A snubby that shoots high is usually fixed with a front sight replacement, because the blade needs to be a little bit taller to force the muzzle down in the sight picture. If the blade is of the replaceable variety, this is usually not a problem, but if the blade is integral to the barrel, it can require costly machining. An alternative is to have the gunsmith build up the tip of the blade by welding, then carefully filing to size and height. This often entails refinishing.

If the gun is shooting just a bit high, it may be cheaper and more expedient to simply experiment with different loads to find one that shoots more closely to the point of aim.

Some thoughts about gold bead sights

The gold bead front sight is a classic for revolver shooters, but not all gold bead sights live up to their potential. Some are downright awful. If you're going to install a gold bead, make sure the surface (face) of the bead itself is flat. Most of them are domed and polished, and that shiny curved surface reflects its surroundings like a mirror, making precision shooting quite difficult — especially in sunny conditions.

In addition to a flat surface, make sure it is treated in such a way to be as non-glare as possible. Ideally it should have matte surface texture, which doesn't reflect back into your eyes and gives a clearer sight picture. This is most easily achieved by bead-blasting the face of the sight with a fine blasting media.

The gold used in the bead has a big effect on how well it shows up in poor lighting conditions. Pure gold has a spectral plot that peaks almost exactly where the human eye is most sensitive. If you've ever panned for gold, you know how even tiny nuggets seem to glow, especially toward dusk! The problem with 24k (pure) gold is that it's very soft and hard to keep inset against the recoil of the snubby. I've found that 22k gold has much of the same spectral properties but tends to hold up better.

To the best of my knowledge, no company makes a gold bead sight that matches these specifications. If you want this classic sight on your snubby and you want it to work well, you'll need to pay a gunsmith to make one for you.

Dehorning

A reality of modern manufacturing is that firearms don't receive much hand finishing. Another reality is that manufacturers don't usually involve experts on things like defensive shooting or concealed carry in the design of their defensive firearms. (There are exceptions, of course, and I've been privileged to be involved with a couple of them.) As a result, the majority of snubbies come out of the factory with sharp edges that make handling in a defensive context painful and, in some cases, actually injurious!

I've cut my fingers on sharp edges and burrs while reloading various revolvers over the years. Sharp hammer spurs can wear on clothing, while crisp corners can tear up leather holsters. Sharp edges and serrations on triggers can quickly abrade away skin on the trigger finger.

The prescription is de-burring the gun: rounding over and polishing out burrs, edges, and corners. This is variously referred to as "dehorning," "melting,", "carry bevel,", and probably other terms I've not yet seen. The process involves a lot of handwork and can be done to a slight or great degree depending on your tastes and the capabilities of the gunsmith. It's not necessary to go to extremes, though. It's sufficient to break and polish the corners and edges without drastically altering the snubby's appearance. As I've often said, a good dehorning is something you should be able to feel but not necessarily see.

The exception is the trigger. The ideal trigger face is noticeably rounded, smooth, and polished so skin is not abraded at all and the finger can slide smoothly over the surface.

Dehorning on a blued gun generally requires refinishing unless you like the "shabby chic" look! Even so, the increase in usability is in my mind worth the investment. (Important note: this modification should not be done on an aluminum gun, as the process requires removal of the anodizing, which protects the aluminum from wear and corrosion.)

Chamfering chambers

A quick and easy modification that helps tremendously with reloading the snubby is to have the chambers chamfered. If you look at the mouths of each chamber on your gun, you'll notice they have a square edge where the flat surface meets the chamber hole. That edge tends to catch on bullet noses and on the edge of the brass case where it wraps around the bullet. It's not much of a snag, mind you, just enough to make reloading the gun a little more awkward and time-consuming than it needs to be.

Chamfering the chamber mouths involves using a special tool to make a 45-degree bevel on the edge of the chamber hole, in effect creating a funnel to guide the new round into the chamber. The amount of metal removed isn't great, but that little bit of bevel makes a huge difference in how easy it is to reload the snubby.

As discussed previously, reloading during a defensive encounter rarely happens. So why make this modification? Because it makes reloading the snubnose revolver easier not just in a defensive shooting, but for your practice as well. It makes handling the gun easier and less annoying, so much so that I've done it to every revolver I've owned regardless of whether any other modifications were done.

HOLSTERS AND CARRY METHODS

As I said at the beginning, the snubnose revolver is the quintessential self-defense firearm. That's the job it was made for and the job it still performs. The snubby is therefore most often carried concealed, and there are almost as many ways to do that as there are people.

Luckily most carry methods fall into some specific categories. Some methods are more optimal than others, and some are downright silly. Let's explore the most common carry methods to keep your snubby close at hand.

Pocket carry

In the front pocket of pants or shorts is probably the primary way most people carry a snubnose revolver today. Pocket carry is unobtrusive, lends itself to a wide range of clothing, tends to be easily accessible, and requires the least change in lifestyle to accommodate the gun. In weather extremes, either hot or cold, pocket carry of a snubnose revolver is a popular option.

It would seem very simple: just drop the gun in your pocket and go. But there's a little more to it.

First, check whether the pocket is suitably sized for carrying a concealed handgun. It needs to be deep enough to conceal the entire snub, including the grips, and wide enough that you can easily withdraw the snubby in a firing grasp when you need it.

Next, check the opening. Many times the opening of the pocket presents a bottleneck or constriction, which makes it very difficult to get the gun out easily. A good test is to put your hand in the pocket, make a fist, then try to remove it rapidly. If you can't do that easily, it's probably not the pocket in which to carry a snubby.

You also need to make sure the pocket doesn't let others easily see inside. I have a pair of khaki shorts that I wear in the summertime, and the front pockets are quite deep and easily hold a snubnose. The problem is that with a gun in the pocket, the top hangs open a bit. Since it's a diagonal slash opening, someone standing behind me can easily look down in the pocket and see the gun!

The pocket itself needs to be made of sturdy material. I have several pairs of nice, conservative summer shorts that have pockets made of very thin material. Were I to carry my snubby in those pockets, it would no doubt wear through that material in short order. Some suit pants are made of similar material, apparently designed to carry little more than a couple of credit cards and a dollar bill or two. Beware of them.

Finally, check the overall fit of the garment. If it's closely fitted, the gun may reveal its outline clearly. The ideal pants have pleats in the front to help mask the outline of the gun, but as long as there's some room in the fit the gun usually just disappears.

Pocket holsters

Allow me to be emphatic: You need a pocket holster! Just dropping the gun into the pocket is not the safe or sane way to carry a snubby!

The pocket holster is an essential part of good pocket carry. First and most importantly, it keeps the snubby in a consistent position and orientation. Carried loose in the pocket, the snubby can turn in various ways, including muzzle up. Imagine needing your snubby in a fight against an attacker and reaching into your pocket only to grab the barrel instead of the grip you expected. That's going to significantly delay (or even stop) your efficient response to the threat. With a proper pocket holster, the snubby is always carried in the same position so you can reach the grip and get a good grasp on the gun quickly and easily.

The pocket holster helps to mask the shape of the gun and make it harder for people to spot the snubby in your pocket. I've done this demonstration with students in class, and it's almost magical how the snubnose disappears when in a holster versus simply shoved into the pocket.

Finally, the pocket holster keeps the gun cleaner. You'd be surprised how much dirt gets into your pockets. In addition to pocket lint, a wide variety of other dirt ends up there as well. The pocket holster provides a barrier between the debris and your gun and prevents foreign material from working its way into the inner parts of the snubby. A cleaner gun works more reliably and lasts longer, and the pocket holster helps keep your gun clean.

It's not just debris, either. A pants pocket is a humid place — especially in warm weather, when pocket carry really comes into its own. A good pocket holster serves as a shield to keep that moisture away from rust-prone parts. (Just because you have a stainless snubby doesn't mean this isn't important to you. Stainless can rust, too, and the springs and other internal parts aren't stainless and certainly can rust.)

A pocket holster isn't a complete rust preventer on its own, but it does keep some of the moisture at bay. For this reason I feel that pocket holsters made of leather, which absorbs moisture and holds it in contact with the gun, are far less preferable than those made from synthetic materials.

It should go without saying, but I'll point out there should be absolutely nothing in that pocket other than the snubby and its holster. Having anything other than the gun in the pocket makes carry unsafe. Not only can other objects work their way into the trigger guard, but your own rustling in the pocket to retrieve other objects increases the risk of knocking the gun out or getting your fingers into contact with the trigger. Never make an exception to this rule!

When shopping for a pocket holster, pay attention to how it fits the gun. You want a fit that's not too tight, as the holster will cling to the gun and the gun will come out of the pocket still attached. At the same time you want just enough fit so the gun doesn't slip around in the holster. If you put the gun into the holster and hold the gun, the holster should not slide off, but if you hold the holster and turn the gun upside-down, the gun should fall out easily. (Do this test with a verified unloaded gun and preferably above a padded surface.)

Also pay attention to how the holster stays in the pocket. Even a properly fitting holster tends to come out of the pocket still on the gun, and any good pocket holster has some method to prevent that happening. Some holsters, like my personal favorite DeSantis Nemesis, have an exterior made of a very tacky rubber substance which grabs onto the pocket material and sticks in the pocket. Other pocket holsters have "wings" that are often shaped a little like a fishhook and are designed to snag on the pocket opening as the gun is withdrawn.

Whatever method the holster uses, make sure there is some provision to keep the holster in the pocket. Drawing a gun and having the holster still attached are quite likely to delay your shooting response significantly — perhaps to the point of uselessness. Make sure the gun comes out of your pocket by itself.

Even those who carry an autoloading pistol for most of the year may find a snubby a better choice during the winter. Wearing a heavy overcoat or a jacket and a raincoat significantly reduces access to a belt-carried pistol. A snubby in a pocket holster, carried in an outside coat pocket, may be the most accessible way of having a concealed defensive handgun in inclement weather.

Belt carry

When most people think of holsters, they visualize a belt holster: one that's worn around the waist. Belt holsters are very popular with more experienced concealed carriers, though I don't encounter a lot of people carrying a snubby on the belt.

OWB and IWB

These two abbreviations divide belt carry into two categories.

OWB stands for Outside the Waist Band, and is the kind of holster most people think of. The OWB holster sits on the outside of the belt and holds the gun in a pouch. The belt usually threads through slots cut in the holster body, though some OWB holsters have loops on the backside through which the belt threads.

The OWB holster is the most comfortable type of belt carry, though at the expense of concealability. Because the OWB holster wants to tilt away from the body, it's dependent on the torsional stiffness of the belt and the holster material to keep the gun upright and snug to the body.

The IWB holster, on the other hand, rides Inside the Waist Band. IWB holsters are worn inside your pants but are attached to the belt with loops or clips. IWB holsters are easily the most concealable belt holster style, but can be less comfortable than OWB styles. They also require that your pants are a size or two larger in order to accommodate the bulk of the gun.

Appendix carry

Appendix carry, sometimes abbreviated AIWB, is an IWB holster worn in front of the body and roughly over the area where your appendix is. Most belt holsters are worn at the peak of the hip (approximately three o'clock, if looking straight ahead is twelve o'clock) or slightly behind. The appendix holster is worn closer to the twelve o'clock position.

AIWB carry has seen a resurgence of popularity in recent years as it's easy to access over a wide range of conditions. But it can be distinctly uncomfortable for some people, requires a specific wardrobe style (untucked shirts are the norm), and necessitates a specific draw and re-holster procedure to be done safely.

The AIWB carry is ideally suited for the snubby's short barrel, and in fact the times I've used this carry method have been with a Smith & Wesson J-Frame carried in a 'City Special' holster by made by Phlster. One significant advantage of appendix carry: You can, by and large, get away with wearing your regular pants size. Unlike on the unyielding hip, the softer abdomen seems to conform around the gun.

If you choose this carry method, be sure that you have a holster specifically designed for AIWB carry. AIWB holsters aren't just regular holsters, but have subtle design changes specifically to make this carry method safer and more comfortable.

Bellybands

The bellyband is one of the most versatile carry methods yet among the least discussed. It's a strip of wide elastic material with a gun pocket either sewn in or attached with hook-and-loop material. It wraps around the torso, secures with a large pad of hook-and-loop material, and relies on the tension of the elastic to keep it in place.

Because it's essentially self-contained, it doesn't need a belt to work — making it ideal for many women's fashions, where strong belts are not the norm. The bellyband can be worn at the waist, where a belt would normally be, and position the gun anywhere from behind the hip to over the appendix.

The bellyband can also be worn higher on the torso. In the days when I had to wear fine suits, I used a bellyband worn at chest level to place a snubby under my left armpit for a shoulder-holster-style draw. (I'm right-handed.) It was totally discreet and one of the few practical ways to carry a defensive firearm in a professional non-permissive environment. Even with the suit jacket off, the gun was completely concealed.

Regardless of your primary carry method, you should have a bellyband in your wardrobe. You will find uses for it.

Shoulder holsters

Who hasn't seen a movie or television cop show where someone toted their gun in a shoulder holster? It's a popular Hollywood carry method because it shows off the gun even in a fairly tight shot of the actor's face, but the shoulder holster has been around even longer than the silver screen. The shoulder holster is one of the few carry methods that is easily accessible if you're sitting, making it popular with truck and taxi drivers.

The problem with the shoulder holster is that even the best examples will print (show their outline) under a suit jacket, and the hanging gun often reveals itself by poking at the covering garment material. From the front, the covering garment needs to be kept closed or restrained in some fashion lest a breeze blow it open and reveal your secret. Drawing from a shoulder holster safely can also be a challenge, which is why many instructors forbid their use in classes.

I carried in a shoulder holster for a time and learned it's really a special-purpose carry method. If you live or work in an environment where you're often sitting, and can wear a heavy enough garment to conceal both the gun and the holster's harness, it may be for you.

Two other caveats: Like a suit, the shoulder holster has to be fitted to you if you expect to achieve maximum concealment. A good one — and you want a good one to get any advantage from it — is also not cheap.

Ankle holsters

The ankle holster should really be called a lower calf holster, but that's not very marketable. It wraps around your leg just above the ankle and is usually secured with hook-and-loop material. Most models also have a strip of strong elastic material to provide the tension needed to keep the holster in place. Concealment is provided by the pant leg.

As you can imagine, the weight of the gun at the end of your leg requires that you practice a bit in order to walk normally. The ankle holster is really suited only to lightweight snubbies, though I have known some very strong people who walked around with an all-steel model on their ankle.

Ankle holsters have many disadvantages. The gun is a long way from your hands; getting to it requires some contortion and bending. Drawing the gun requires the use of both hands: one to pull up the pant leg, and the other to draw the gun. The gun will reveal itself if you cross your legs, and depending on the cut of your trousers, it may be visible to someone below you on stairs or escalators.

The draw from a standing position is slow and requires a lot of flexibility. Finally, ankle carry exposes the gun to a greater amount of dirt than almost every other carry method, which is why even hardcore semiauto pistol users revert to the more reliable snubby for ankle carry.

On the plus side, the ankle holster — if worn on the inside of the weak-side leg — is often more easily accessible from a sitting position than all but the shoulder holster. For instance, if you drive a vehicle with an upright seating position (such as a truck or SUV), it may be among the fastest to access. It may be an option for people with driving jobs, but for almost anyone else, I recommend staying away from the flawed ankle holster.

Off-body carry

Off-body carry, often abbreviated OBC, is a catch-all term for carry methods that aren't attached to your body in some way. Purses are the most common OBC method, but the term also applies to briefcases, backpacks, and all manner of hand-carried firearm containers. Off-body carry is particularly popular with women, whose fashions often make concealed carry difficult or impossible. A gun in the purse is one way to get around the constraints imposed by fashionable clothing.

Off-body carry is also convenient and comfortable, regardless of your gender. Pick up your bag or case, and you have your gun. You don't have to worry about printing or picking the right concealment garment. Many people new to concealed carry find this an approachable carry method. But OBC has significant enough issues that I normally do not recommend the practice.

The problems with off-body carry

First, it's much slower to access the gun than all but perhaps the ankle holster. It almost always requires two hands to access the gun. There are exceptions, but one hand generally has to hold the container (for lack of a better word) while the other hand accesses the gun.

You have to be careful that the container is always carried in the same spot and in the same orientation. For instance, if you're carrying in a purse that has gun access on one side, you have to make sure that side is always in the same place relative to your shooting (strong) hand. If you pick it up and put it on the right shoulder when you're used to it being on the left, your access is going to be significantly slowed from its normally slow pace.

The most significant downside to OBC, as I see it, is that from a safety and security aspect the container becomes the gun. Because it's not attached to your body you will, at some point, need to put it down — at which time anyone and everyone has access to your firearm. I've read many news reports of children getting to their mom's purse, finding her gun, and shooting themselves (or sometimes Mommy herself).

Theft target

With OBC, you must keep constant watch over the container just as you would if you left the bare gun in the same spot. Sooner or later your attention to the container will wane, and that's a dangerous time for someone to come across it.

Of course the container itself is a theft target at all times. Hundreds of thousands of women's purses are stolen every year in this country. Identity theft is the goal, and it's extremely common. If you're carrying a gun in that purse you stand a very good chance of having it taken along with your credit cards.

It's not just theft, either. Check with your local mall's lost and found and see how many purses, bags, satchels, duffels, and other such containers are left behind on a regular basis. Not only do you need to be sure someone isn't taking the bag you just put down, you have to make sure you don't walk away and forget it!

That being said, I do think OBC is a viable carry method under a very small percentage of very specific circumstances. If your wardrobe or environment is such that you simply can't carry your snubby on your person, OBC may be a consideration — but only after you've exhausted all other options. The downsides of off-body carry are so great it should be considered a last resort.

If you choose off-body carry, you absolutely must:

1) Practice retrieving and shooting from the container. The mechanics of drawing the gun safely and efficiently are very different than any other method

and need to be practiced.

2) Commit to carrying the container in the same orientation, position, and manner every time you pick it up.

3) Use only a container with a separate compartment for your snubby. The gun must be held in a fixed position by a holster, and absolutely nothing else is allowed in that space.

4) Be sure you can access the gun without setting the container down.

5) Lock the container away whenever you are not in physical contact with it. Yes, this means if you're in public, you can never let it out of your reach and sight.

6) Never leave the container unsecured at home or allow children any access to it. Hiding it on a high shelf does not count.

Off-body carry is a very specialized carry method for very specific circumstances and requires explicit procedures to make it workable and safe. In the end, it's probably better to find some sort of on-body carry method that works with your wardrobe and lifestyle!

DRAWING FROM CONCEALMENT

The snubnose revolver has always been a personal protection tool. It was conceived first and foremost to be carried. The shortened barrel not only made it easy to conceal, but also easy to get into action quickly when needed.

At the same time, getting the snubby out of its holster and into a position where it can be fired effectively is a primary defensive shooting skill. If you're going to carry your snubby to protect yourself or your loved ones, developing a reliable and efficient draw is one of your most important goals.

You've learned about the drawstroke in a previous chapter. How do you put that to use under realistic conditions? Because your snubby is more than likely to be carried concealed, getting to the gun is a little more complicated than it is when you're on the range with the gun in the open. How do you deal with the added complication of the cover clothing?

Focus on the basics

I've been to more than one defensive shooting class where the instructor made a big deal out of how to draw from under concealment. Some of them go to the extreme of suggesting you modify jackets and overshirts by sewing weights into the corners, so they can be more efficiently "thrown" away from the gun. I admit, in my early years, that I bought into that line of thinking.

Learn from my mistake. It's not necessary to spend time testing whether it's faster to have the fingers of your hand straight or cupped as you use them to clear your cover garment from the gun. (One class I took spent the better part of an hour testing which method was best — a waste of valuable training resources.)

I think it's better to build on motions and habits you're used to using in the rest of your life. What do I mean by that?

Think about how you get your wallet or car keys out when you need them. When you reach into your hip pocket for your wallet, for instance, do you obsess about how to get past your jacket or shirt? At the risk of using a clichéd phrase, you just do it! You reach under your coat and into your pocket without really worrying about the process. It's something you probably do every day, perhaps even multiple times a day, and I'll bet you never stood in front of a mirror to learn how to do it (let alone sewn weights into your jacket to make it faster).

I suggest you think about how to draw your gun in the same way. Focus not on clearing your cover garments, but instead on getting your hand onto the gun in a solid shooting grasp. The key is getting your hand to your snubby as efficiently as you can without grabbing any clothing along the way. Once you've got a solid grasp on the gun, bring it out of the holster, orient it on the target, extend through the ready position, touch the trigger, and fire the shot.

Think about getting your hand onto your gun, and the rest takes care of itself.

What if you need both hands?

Some carry methods and some covering garments might require you to use two hands to access your snubby. In some cases it can be done with only one hand, but is much easier and faster using two. My recommendation is to avoid carry methods which require both hands, as you might not have both hands free to get to the gun.

If you covering garments are such that using one hand is possible but using both is significantly faster or easier, I'll suggest first that you consider changing into something that is more easily accessed with just one hand. I realize that it's very easy to say that, and I acknowledge that it isn't always possible.

I do recommend practicing accessing your snubby with one hand most of the time. Having only one hand available is the "worst case" scenario, and being proficient is better than practicing for the best case. Having two hands available seems easy in comparison, and I've found that proficiency in the more difficult condition translates easily to the less difficult — but it doesn't seem to work in reverse.

The rule is still to get your hand to the gun as efficiently as possible. If that means using two hands, and you have both available, then by all means do so. Be sure, though, to practice for those situations where you can't.

What about snagging the gun?

You'll hear quite a bit about the possibility of snagging the gun and delaying or even fouling the drawstroke. In fact much of the justification for exaggerated "clearing" movements is to prevent the gun from snagging as it's drawn from the holster. I've never found that to be helpful, at least not with normal clothing; it just immediately falls back on top of the gun as it's coming out of the holster.

Is snagging a real issue with the snubnose? That depends largely on the particular model. The point on which the average snubby will snag is the hammer spur. Some snubbies, like the Colt Detective Special, have a particularly sharp fishhook profile that seems to grab clothing more aggressively than some others. Of course concealed-hammer snubby designs, like the Smith & Wesson Bodyguard and Centennial series, are virtually snag-free no matter what the carry method is.

How the snubby is carried is also a factor. Drawn from a belt holster, for instance, I've never found snagging to be a big issue with any snubnose revolver. From a pocket holster, however, snagging is almost guaranteed with any snubby that has an exposed hammer spur. Some deep carry methods, such as the bellyband worn under a shirt on the weak side as described in the section on Holsters and Carry Methods, will also cause the hammer spur to snag. For that reason, I only recommend pocket and deep carry for snubbies that have enclosed or hidden hammers, such as the aforementioned Smith & Wesson models.

Do sights snag?
In the 1970s a new rear sight design for autoloading pistols came on the market, a design that purported to reduce snagging on the rear sight. Aside from being sloped in the wrong direction to prevent snagging on the draw, the sight addressed a non-existent issue. I've never experienced any hangup from clothing snagging on the adjustable sights found on snubbies such as the Smith & Wesson Model 60 carried in a belt holster. As with the autoloading pistols, I think the sights are the least of your worries.

Pocket and deep carry methods pose a different issue. For those uses, I suggest only snubbies that have fixed sights, which are generally non-snag by design.

Modifying the snubby to reduce snagging

If you're going to carry your snubnose revolver in a pocket holster or a deep-carry method and you don't have one of the concealed hammer models, you can have your gun modified for the role.

A common modification to eliminate snagging on the hammer spur is to eliminate the spur itself. A gunsmith can cut off the hammer spur and refinish the hammer so its appearance doesn't suffer from the surgery. If you elect to have this done you'll need to test the gun thoroughly afterwards, as reducing the mass of the hammer can result in ignition issues. The Colt Detective Special, Agent, and Cobra snubbies are particularly sensitive to this. If you've had reduced-effort springs installed, this is more likely to be a problem than if the springs are stock.

Another method is to install a hammer shroud, which screws onto the frame of the gun. This requires a gunsmith to drill and tap holes in the appropriate locations for the shroud to attach. Once the shroud is in place the hammer is largely covered, enough that clothing shouldn't pose an issue.

At this writing, Waller and Sons, the only manufacturer of hammer shrouds for Colt and Smith & Wesson J-Frame revolvers, appears to be out of business, but some sources online still have them in stock.

Dry practicing your drawstroke

Dry practice, covered in detail in a separate chapter, is a great way to work on your drawstroke from the various sorts of clothing you might wear. Practicing getting your hand to the gun and drawing it to extension without actually shooting will help you refine your movements. This is probably the very best use for dry practice, in fact!

Be sure to practice with both business and casual wear. If pocket carry is your choice, practice with all the pants (or coats, if you carry in a coat pocket) you are likely to wear. Even small variations in the pocket opening, pocket width, and pocket depth have a significant impact on getting your hand to the gun and then getting your hand and the gun out of the pocket.

If you have more than one holster, practice with all of them. You may find that some holsters are less than ideal in one aspect or another of their design, and dry practice is the best way to discover that. I've found many holsters that seemed fine until I tried to rapidly grasp the gun. The area around the grip wasn't enough to get my fingers in and around the gun, which slowed the draw considerably.

Dry practice will reveal these kinds of problems.

HOME DEFENSE

It's true that the snubnose revolver was always intended as an arm of personal safety. It's the revolver that can be carried with you easily and in comfort, ready to use to defend yourself from the attack you didn't know was coming. It has always, therefore, been a concealed carry piece — even before the term concealed carry was coined!

Seen in that light, it might be odd to talk about using the snubby as a home defense tool, but many people over many generations have used one for just that job. While the snubby's vices (low capacity, difficult to shoot well) would seem to work against it in the home protection role, it can still be pressed into service. After all, having a gun that is not ideal for the task but is familiar to you is preferable to one that is perfect for the job but with which you're not as skilled.

Carry at home

Over the years I've said this hundreds, if not thousands, of times: the only safe places for your defensive firearm are on your person or secured against unauthorized access. When we talk about home defense those are the only two responsible options. For some reason, though, many people who routinely carry outside their home take the gun off when they walk in their front door.

Your first line of defense can and probably should be the same concealed carry snubby you have during the rest of the day. Not just because it's more readily at hand than a properly secured gun, but because it's in a place you're already familiar with.

Your home itself provides a layer of protection on which, whether you realize it or not, you rely. What about when you're outside your home but still on your property? You might be loading or unloading your car in the driveway, weeding the flower bed next to the street, or walking out to the mailbox. In all those cases, you probably feel at ease because you're still technically at home, but you're actually in a transitional space: between hard protection (the house) and a public area (the street).

On top of that, you're a very long way from your stored defensive firearm and likely also beyond your early warning system. If you're attacked in that transition area, you'll likely not see it coming and not be prepared, tool-wise, to efficiently deal with the threat.

Do attacks happen in those transition areas? Yes, they do. Carjackings from driveways are common in many areas, and opportunistic attackers coming off the street to take advantage of an unwary homeowner are not unheard of. The concealed carry snubby has as much value at home as it does anywhere else. Perhaps, because of the tendency to let our guard down at home, it has even more value!

My first recommendation, then, is to conceal carry your snubby while you're at home. Even if you don't (or can't) carry a defensive firearm outside the home, on your own property you are almost universally allowed to (this is not legal advice, and of course you must check your local laws on this matter).

If you do carry your snubby in public, you may need to make some changes to your carry system between your work and leisure wardrobes. Reading the section on Holsters and Carry Methods will help you with the differences and your choices. Those who slip into sweatpants at home, for example, will be well served by one of the bellyband options that work without a heavy belt.

Stored yet ready for action

You can't carry at home all the time; at some point the snubby has to come off your person and be stored somewhere. I strongly suggest a modern quick-access safe or lock box for this purpose. I covered quick-access safes in the section on Storage, but now I want to talk about the devices as part of a total home defense response plan.

The benefits of the quick-access safe are, as the name implies, security and safety combined with fast access in the event of an emergency. I recommend storing your home-defense handgun in such a safe if you have children, if other children visit occasionally, or if you routinely have non-authorized people in your home.

(By "non-authorized," I don't mean bad people or people with criminal records. The term simply refers to those you haven't personally vetted for their ability to properly and safely handle firearms, or those whose responsibility is not known. The ability to keep unauthorized users, including children, away from a deadly weapon is one of the biggest reasons to have a quick-access safe.)

Regardless of the exact nature of storage, it's important to keep the home-defense gun in the same place and same relative position at all times. Rolling around loose in a nightstand drawer qualifies for the first but not the second; every time the drawer is opened, the gun can move around. A better choice, if the nightstand drawer is appropriate, is to keep it in a form-fitting box inside the drawer. The box should be held in a fixed position, and duct tape is an easy way to make sure that it is..

How to stage the snubnose

I'm going to suggest something the rest of the gun world considers radical, perhaps even heretical: Keep the snubby with a speedloader inserted into the cylinder, but without the rounds being released into the chambers. The reason for this is twofold. First, the gun in the storage container is out of your possession. You don't know for a fact that it's loaded.

You could open the cylinder, look, and close the cylinder again — but what if it's dark, which it's likely to be if you need it? I'd rather pick the gun up, load it myself, and know it's ready to go. Having the speedloader inserted simply requires you to release the rounds and close the cylinder, which is at least as fast as opening, checking, and then closing. The time factor is a wash.

Second, if you've been awakened in the middle of the night, you're likely to be disoriented for a minute or so. The extra cognitive steps of releasing the ammunition and closing the cylinder are two extra things you need to take before you start pulling the trigger. That little bit of time and brain engagement gives you the chance to process the sensory information you're gathering and determine if you really do have an attacker — or if it's your wayward teenager coming in later than expected.

As this is being written I've reviewed four separate news stories, all happening in the last month, where someone shot a person they thought was a home invader but turned out to be someone else: a friend (two cases), their own child (one case), and a significant other who came home unexpectedly early. Three of them resulted in fatalities. These are cases that might not have happened had there been something to engage the brain before putting a loaded firearm in the hand of a groggy person.

Finally, it's likely to be dark when you discover you might need your snubnose. Opening a box in the dark and needing to get your hands on a loaded gun increase the risk of accidentally depressing the trigger and firing an unintentional shot, which is dangerous. Having the snubby unloaded makes it safer for the initial contact and handling. By the time you're in a position to release the rounds from the speedloader you should have the snubby in a firm shooting grasp. You'll also have it pointed in a generally safe direction, giving you complete control over the gun.

Where should the box be located?

I suggest your quick-access safe be located near your own bed. This is the place you'd likely need it if someone broke into your house and managed to get past your deterrents (dogs) and alarm system while you were asleep. Your bedroom is also likely your barricade space: the defensible room to which you'd retreat if you realized someone was trying to break in. It makes sense to have your non-carried gun in that area.

The safe needs to be secured so someone can't grab it and walk off with it easily. The quick-access safe isn't a theft deterrent like a full-size safe, but at the same time you don't want to make it an easy target for someone who happens to spot the box. Models are available in both horizontal configuration (secure to the floor underneath the bed) or vertical (screw into a wall stud). Securing the box not only makes it a little harder to steal, but it also defeats many of the procedures that can possibly bypass the locking mechanism.

For those with children living at home, renowned trainer Rob Pincus makes the suggestion that your child's room be the barricade space, and your safe be secured in the closet of that room. Many consider this a radical proposal, but he points out that if someone breaks into your house, protecting your children will probably be your first thought. If your barricade space is your room, that would mean going to their room, possibly exposing yourself to the intruder, then going back to your room — exposing both (or all) of you to danger.

Making the child's room your defensible space means you only need to make only one trip. (I should point out that you do not give the child authorized access to the safe!)

If you have children, I strongly recommend you store a high-intensity lithium-powered flashlight in the safe with your gun. Children are intensely curious, and if you think back to your early childhood you probably remember going through everything that was in your house! Very few kids could resist playing with a flashlight next to the quick-access safe, and you could find the batteries dead at the least opportune time. Having a light of known condition inside the safe is a reasonable precaution, and at the cost of lithium batteries might actually save you money in the long run.

If you have a gun, you also need an early warning system

"But what if I wake up and the bad guy is at the foot of my bed? That extra step is going to delay my defense and I might end up dead!"

Surprise attacks certainly happen and make for a seemingly compelling argument but, without turning this into a home-defense book, let me stress that your snubby can't be your only line of protection. Not every situation is a shooting situation, and therefore not every self-defense incident needs the gun. Remember the old saying, "If your only tool is a hammer, every problem looks like a nail"? The same thing applies to having a gun for home defense with no other provisions for overall security.

If you have a gun for home and family protection, you also need an early warning system to alert you to the presence of something out of the ordinary. That something might be a criminal intruder, but then again it might not be. The early warning system gives you time to figure out the difference and put your protection plan into action. Without that, your only recourse is to always go to the gun — even when it might not be the right response.

Early warning systems can be as sophisticated as a complex alarm or as simple as a dog that barks whenever it senses someone who shouldn't be there.

Early warning systems in action
Here's how the combination might work: you're sound asleep when your dog starts barking. You're jolted out of your sleep, groggy and disoriented, and as your mind clears, you realize something is out of the ordinary. You reach into your gun storage space and retrieve a high-intensity flashlight, which you shine through the doorway of your bedroom. You see nothing, but the dog seems convinced someone is there.

Your mind is now starting to engage as you pick up your snubby and release the speedloader you inserted when you stored the gun. The rounds drop the rest of the way into their chambers and you know the gun is loaded as you close the cylinder.

Keeping the muzzle pointed in a safe direction, you shine the light down the hallway and see the emerging figure of … your teenage son who got off his night-shift job early and didn't want to wake you. So he walked silently and didn't turn on any lights — two behaviors that put Rover on alert.

Now imagine the same scenario, except you don't have any early warning system or response plan. You're still trying to wipe the sleep out of your eyes as you're surprised by the shadow moving down the hallway, and you have a loaded gun in your hand …

That's how tragedies occur. Make sure you have some sort of early warning system to go along with your gun. In fact, I suggest that you get the system before you get the gun!

Retrieving the snubby

Like drawing the gun for concealed carriers, retrieving your snubnose and getting it into a condition to be used is a skill you need to train and practice. I recommend practicing two slightly different scenarios: when you're in bed, as if you've been awakened by an intruder; and when you're somewhere else in the house and are forced to run to the barricade space to retrieve the gun.

This is easily done in "dry practice," without ammunition. You need some plastic dummy rounds, which are brightly colored (usually orange or yellow) ammunition facsimiles used for training. They're available at most well-stocked gun stores and big box outdoor retailers.

First, clear the snubby, making sure there is no live ammunition anywhere in the room. Take any live ammunition you find and put it in another area of the house, then close the door to your safe room. Insert the dummy rounds into your speedloader, then stage the gun and fake ammunition just as you do with real ammo. Now you can practice loading the snubby with a dramatically lessened chance of an unintentional shot.

The exercise is simple: Get to the quick-access safe, open it, release the rounds from the speedloader, close the cylinder, and grab your flashlight. Keeping the gun pointed in a safe direction, you can now practice lighting the area where a bad guy might make entry, mimic calling 911, giving commands to the intruder that the police have been called, and so on. It's important to practice this in the dark whenever possible to duplicate the conditions under which you're likely to use those skills.

Also practice getting to the barricade space from other rooms in the house, and don't forget to include the bathroom in that scenario. Many people don't think of an intruder showing up while they're getting out of the shower, or worse — while sitting on the toilet!

If you have children, practice getting them from their bedroom to the safe space. The mechanics of doing this are beyond the scope of this book, but a good resource is *Defend Yourself: A Comprehensive Security Plan for the Armed Homeowner* by Rob Pincus.

FINAL WORDS

Some years back, I quipped that the snubnose revolver is the easiest gun to shoot but the most difficult to shoot well. I've also been known to say that the snubby revolver is an "expert's gun." That is to say, shooting a snubby well in a defensive context requires some dedication on the part of its owner. I don't want the statements to scare you off but rather to challenge you to become an expert yourself!

Developing the skills to efficiently shoot your snubby in a defensive encounter will help your shooting skills with any handgun you pick up. Once you've overcome its limitations and challenges, everything else seems easy by comparison.

Maybe that's why some of us continue to carry the snubby even in this day of compact high-capacity autoloaders. I hope this book has given you some idea of both the snubby's capabilities and what you can do to maximize your snubnose shooting skills!

ALSO BY GRANT CUNNINGHAM

Handgun Training - Practice Drills For Defensive Shooting

Defensive Revolver Fundamentals

Defensive Pistol Fundamentals

Gun Digest Book Of The Revolver

Shooter's Guide To Handguns

FREE SELF DEFENSE RESOURCES

Save money and shoot more — download and print out my FREE defensive training targets at home!

www.grantcunningham.com/free-snubnose-targets/

Every week on my blog I share news and information about self defense and personal security. From defensive shooting to situational awareness, I cover it all!

Subscribe for free and get my blog posts directly to your email box!

www.grantcunningham.com/news-views

ABOUT THE AUTHOR

Grant Cunningham is a renowned author and teacher in the areas of self defense, personal safety, home and family defense, and instructor development. (As well as being an internationally known — but retired — gunsmith.) He's been a fan of the snubnose for many years and often carries one for personal defense.

He has written several popular books on handguns and defensive shooting, including *The Gun Digest Book of the Revolver, Shooter's Guide to Handguns, Defensive Revolver Fundamentals, Defensive Pistol Fundamentals,* and *Handgun Training: Practice Drills for Defensive Shooting*. He's also written articles on shooting, self defense, training and teaching for many magazines and shooting websites, including *Concealed Carry Magazine, Gun Digest Magazine,* the *Association of Defensive Shooting Instructors* (ADSI), and the *Personal Defense Network*.

Grant has been featured or profiled in the Complete Book of Handguns, *The Accurate Rifle* magazine, and *Custom Combat Handguns* magazine. He's the host of the *Defensive Revolver Fundamentals DVD* from the National Rifle Association's Personal Firearm Defense series and of the upcoming PDN production *Using the Bullpup Rifle for Home and Personal Defense*.

He's trained with many nationally known instructors, including Massad Ayoob, Rob Pincus, Gila Hayes, Marty Hayes, Andy Stanford, Clyde Caceres, as well as regionally known instructors. Grant holds instructor certifications from I.C.E. Training (Combat Focus Shooting, Combat Focus Carbine, and Home Defense Handgun), as well as an NRA Instructor certificate. In addition, he was a founding member of the Association of Defensive Shooting Instructors (ADSI).

Grant teaches workshops all over the United States in self protection, home and family defense, and defensive shooting. You can find his workshop schedule at:

www.grantcunningham.com

You can also find him hosting Personal Defense Network's twice-monthly webcast, *Training Talk*.

Grant has been endorsed by some prominent members of the defensive training community and the firearms industry, such as:

"...you can take Grant's advice to the bank." — *Massad Ayoob*

"Grant is an established expert, and has been for many years. [...] he can distill the essence of a concept from a cumbersome explanation and efficiently get a student to grasp the important principles." — *Rob Pincus*

49796194R00121

Made in the USA
San Bernardino, CA
05 June 2017